Praise for *Educating wi*

"*Educating with Passion and Purpose* is a .... to resources on teacher wellness. The authors' perso.... stories are relatable and will provide insight for readers into their own desires to contribute meaningfully to education."

—Elena Aguilar, author of
Onward: Cultivating Emotional Resilience in Educators

"For nearly 15 years I've learned alongside Meredith and Rebekah, and I continue to learn from them through the pages of this book. They interweave their personal journeys with practical tips for educators in a way that truly gets to the heart of the matter: it's all about purpose. Teacher educators, teachers, and school leaders alike will identify, reflect, and improve their practice by engaging with the personal stories and reflective prompts in this book."

—Kristen Hawley Turner, PhD,
Professor and Director of Teacher Education, Drew University

"This book is truly an inspiration to anyone fortunate enough to read it. The insightful advice, relatable experiences shared, and the encouragement and resources offered to overcome obstacles make it applicable and useful for all educators—at any level in their careers. Through tears, smiles, and head nods in agreement, there is no doubt that this book will help unlock your 'why' and motivate you to grow as an educator."

—Shelby Sprung,
Special education teacher, P94m

"Teachers, leaders, and anyone who works in education will benefit from *Educating with Passion and Purpose: Keep the Fire Going without Burning Out*. The stories, wisdom, and reflective activities will support educators to sustain and evolve throughout their career."

—Alexis Goldberg,
Managing Director of School Support, The Urban Assembly

"Reading Meredith's and Rebekah's stories reminded me not only of what I loved about learning in the classroom everyday with students, but also that this daily work is something I believe to be sacrosanct and the leader's duty to support and protect. When you are a district leader, it's easy to get caught up in the daily political and operational work that doesn't feel quite so sacred; reading their powerful narratives has inspired me to reconnect to my 'why' and to try and ground my daily work more explicitly with it in mind. This book could not have come at a better time."

—Carolyn Yaffe,
Executive Director of Valley Charter Schools, California

"With the engaging voices of experienced teachers and leaders, the authors provide an insightful and pragmatic guide for educators who are questioning their purpose or facing burnout."

—Marshall A. George,
Olshan Professor of Clinical Practice at Hunter College
of the City University of New York

"Rebekah and Meredith provide a candid look at preventing and healing from teacher burnout and do so through personal storytelling that will draw you in in a deeply captivating way and will provide current and future educators with specific and equitable strategies to combat a very real problem in our field. Educators at all levels should pick up this book and learn from the infinite wisdom!"

—Carlos Beato, EdD,
Co-Director of Next Generation Learning Challenges

"In the midst of a national teacher shortage, Matson and Shoaf provide a critical contribution to the discussion about how we retain, sustain, and reinvigorate educators—by reconnecting with their purpose! Educators from the district office to the classroom should take note of these practical ideas for transforming experience and avoiding burnout."

—Jeffrey Garrett,
Founder of JM Garrett Learning Group
and Senior Vice President of Leadership Development,
Partnership for Los Angeles Schools

"In *Educating with Passion and Purpose*, Matson and Shoaf combine their extensive experience to create an invaluable resource for teachers and the leaders who support them. This book combines the power of personal narrative with practical reflection exercises and resources to help teachers build careers, curriculums, and communities grounded in purpose and filled with passion."

—Ivelisse Ramos Brannon,
Former high school English teacher,
Curricular consultant, and PhD student at Harvard University

"A thoughtful, heartfelt, and comprehensive guide—I'll be giving to every teacher I know."

—Jessica Murnane,
author of *One Part Plant and Know Your Endo*

"With compelling personal narratives and a plethora of practical suggestions, these veteran teacher-leaders provide educators at all levels practical
and valuable examples of how to maintain energy and commitment in the
classroom. Given the post-COVID education landscape, this book is
required reading for everyone working in schools."

—Bil Johnson,
Retired public school teacher educator and author of
The Student-Centered Classroom Handbook and Right Time, Right Places

Educating with Passion and Purpose

To Victoria!

Educating with Passion and Purpose

Keep the Fire Going without Burning Out

Re-ignite Your Passion!
Meredith

Meredith Matson

Rebekah Shoaf

Prioritize ♡♡ R your Purpose!

JB JOSSEY-BASS™

A Wiley Brand

Published by Jossey-Bass

A Wiley Brand
111 River St., Hoboken NJ 07030
www.josseybass.com

Printed in the United States of America
Published simultaneously in Canada

Jossey-Bass books and products are available through most bookstores. To contact Jossey-Bass directly call
our Customer Care Department within the U.S. at 800-956-7739, outside the U.S. at 317-572-3986, or fax
317-572-4002.

Wiley publishes in a variety of print and electronic formats and by print-on-demand. Some material
included with standard print versions of this book may not be included in e-books or in print-on-demand.

If this book refers to media such as a CD or DVD that is not included in the version you purchased, you may
download this material at http://booksupport.wiley.com.

For more information about Wiley products, visit www.wiley.com.

Library of Congress Cataloging-in-Publication Data

Names: Matson, Meredith, author. | Shoaf, Rebekah, author.
Title: Educating with passion and purpose : keep the fire going without
   burning out / Meredith Matson, Rebekah Shoaf.
Description: Hoboken, NJ : Jossey-Bass, 2023. | Includes index.
Identifiers: LCCN 2023007772 (print) | LCCN 2023007773 (ebook) | ISBN
   9781119893615 (paperback) | ISBN 9781119893622 (adobe pdf) | ISBN
   9781119893639 (epub)
Subjects: LCSH: Teaching--Psychological aspects. | Teachers—Job
   satisfaction. | Teacher turnover—Prevention. | Burn out
   (Psychology)—Prevention.
Classification: LCC LB1027 .M363 2023 (print) | LCC LB1027 (ebook) | DDC
   371.1001/9—dc23/eng/20230223
LC record available at https://lccn.loc.gov/2023007772
LC ebook record available at https://lccn.loc.gov/2023007773

Cover Design: Wiley
Cover Image: © White Bear Studio/Getty Images

SKY10044355_031523

For our first teachers:
Our families.
And our forever teachers:
Our students.

Contents

Introduction

> "It was honestly great to feel understood. When
> a teacher is just as eager to learn about you as
> they are to teach, I feel like there is a bond and
> mutual respect, which makes it easier for both
> students and teachers."
>
> —Leianna, Class of 2017

Why We Wrote This Book

When the COVID-19 pandemic began in March 2020, our lives,
like everyone else's, were thrown into upheaval. New York City
was ground zero for the initial wave of the pandemic, and we
were both locked down inside our homes, Rebekah in the South
Bronx, and Meredith nearby in Baldwin, Long Island. As we
struggled to maintain some semblance of normalcy in our
personal and professional lives, we checked in with each other
remotely. One day that April, Meredith texted Rebekah, "I still
dream about our book." She was referring to the book we'd
started talking about writing years earlier, when we were teacher
leaders and coaches together during the 2012–2013 school year.
We'd periodically talked about cowriting a book about our
experiences as mid-career educators, but life had gotten in the
way, and we never took it any further. In April 2020, however,
we had nothing but time. We started writing on our own and
then meeting weekly online to read and discuss each other's
work. We spent the entire first two years of the pandemic writing
together. Many people had pandemic projects. This was ours.

Originally, we thought we were writing a book about how to
prevent and heal teacher burnout. However, as we wrote, we
discovered that actually we were writing a book about purpose.
We realized the key to avoiding burnout and recovering from it
over the course of our own careers has been having a strong

sense of why we are educators in the first place. We came to understand that when you are able to stand in your purpose, you can use that purpose as a litmus test for decision-making to ensure you are actually living and working in alignment with your purpose. We've found that burnout generally stems from a misalignment around purpose, and educators can prevent and heal burnout by rekindling, reconnecting, and recommitting to their purpose.

Our own purpose in this book is to help other educators uncover how to maintain a long, productive, inspired career in education. Through stories from our own careers over a combined four decades as teachers and leaders, as well as reflective activities to help you think about your own journeys and experiences, you'll learn how to stay connected to your *why*: your dynamic sense of purpose as an educator. You'll learn to uncover and nourish your own *why* and how to keep that purpose close when all of the things that lead to burnout start to separate you from it.

We want to reinforce that we're sharing our stories to illustrate what this reflective work has looked like in our own lives, not as instructive case studies of what we think you should do. We share our experiences not because we think they're universal but because we know they're real. You have your own real experiences in your own real context, and we hope our stories provide examples that give you new ways to think about the choices you're making in your personal and professional life. We've spent our education careers in urban communities, and we were both high school humanities teachers, but the reflective work that we've done ourselves, that we're supported other educators in doing, and that we're inviting you to do is applicable for educators in all grades, subjects, and settings.

Who This Book Is For

While this book is for individual educators and the leaders who support them, we want to acknowledge there are structural factors that lead to educator burnout. We strongly support the systemic changes necessary to transform the profession into a sustainable lifelong career option, especially in the schools and districts where the demands on teachers and leaders are particularly Herculean. However, this book is for the people who need support right now and can't wait for the often-protracted pace of systemic change, so we focus on actions that individual educators can take to improve their own working conditions and quality of life. We are grateful for the work that researchers, labor unions, and other advocacy organizations are doing to fight for the systemic changes that will impact all educators and students for the better. We also recognize that, while the pandemic exacerbated the factors that contribute to burnout, many of those factors long preexisted the pandemic. We believe reflection on and connection to purpose is the way forward for individual educators in the context of challenges both directly related to and beyond the pandemic.

We're especially interested in engaging with educators who are in the early-to-middle stages of their careers. Much of what we share in this book is advice we wish we'd received as preservice and beginning teachers, as well as when we were at crucial career crossroads, including burnout periods. If you are new to the profession, supporting those who are, or considering whether to continue in the profession, we hope you find stories and activities here to help you maintain a long, productive, and sustainable career in education. Teachers have the best jobs on the planet but also the hardest ones. Most of us can't do it on our own or without a strategy for how to make it through the tough days, weeks, and years. We want all students to have happy, healthy teachers, but that can't happen if teachers don't have opportunities to reflect, heal, and reorient around their sense of purpose so their students are at the center of their work, which is why we start each chapter with a quote by one of our own current or former students. At the same time, our goal is not to keep all educators in the classroom no matter what. Rather, we want all educators to understand and live in alignment with their own sense of purpose, whatever that is.

We also want to emphasize that we are not mental health professionals. If you are in crisis, please seek professional help for the sake of your loved ones, your students, and your colleagues, as well as yourself.

How to Use This Book

In each chapter, we share our own reflective process with respect to the chapter's subject, followed by prompts and activities designed for all educators (the "Your Turn" sections) and then the "Additional Considerations for Leaders" in particular. Our goal in sharing our own experiences is to make our thinking visible, as we've worked through these same reflective prompts and activities in our time as teachers and leaders.

We hope our examples help illustrate the essential, rewarding, and messy process of reflective engagement we have undertaken and continue to work through two decades into our careers in education. However, if our stories don't resonate with you or you'd prefer to jump right into practice and application for your own experiences and context, feel free to skip to the "Your Turn" sections of each chapter, as well as the reproducibles in the appendix and at http://www.wiley.com/go/educatingpassion purpose.

In Chapters 1 and 2, we focus on the process of uncovering your purpose and what can happen when your actions and experiences aren't aligned with your purpose: burnout. In the remaining chapters, we focus on how to make decisions aligned with your purpose so you can maintain a sustainable future in the profession and prevent burnout moving forward. By staying connected to your *why*, you can figure out for yourself when to say "yes" and "no" in all the right ways.

As educators ourselves, we know everyone learns in different ways, so please engage with the "Your Turn" activities in the ways that will be most resonant and effective for you. Here are a few possibilities:

◆ Read the reflective prompts, pause, and respond to them in your head.

◆ Write out your responses on paper or your device.

◆ Keep a separate journal or blog while you read this book and write your responses there.

◆ Record voice memos or videos on your phone or elsewhere for private use.

◆ Record voice memos or videos and post them on a platform of your choice to share with your community.

◆ Share and discuss your responses with a book group, professional team, or other reading community.

◆ Work through the book with an existing professional learning community (PLC) or a new one created just for this purpose. Read a chapter a week, select prompts and activities to work through independently and collaboratively, share your reflections, and develop community commitments to next steps.

◆ Work through the reproducibles, either in the book or via the downloads at https://www.wiley.com/go/educating passionpurpose.

Why Reflection Matters

Committing to a long, productive, sustainable career as an educator while maintaining your personal health and relationships, as well as fulfilling your nonprofessional goals and dreams, is long, hard work. We do not believe you'll be able to leave burnout in your rearview mirror forever by simply reading this book and completing all of the reflective activities. Rather, the work of staying connected and committed to your purpose is an ongoing, iterative process we continuously return to on our journeys as educators, especially because for so many of us the reasons why we became educators are at odds with what today's educational institutions expect from us and our students. We believe educators have the most difficult jobs in our society, and that work requires time for reflection, especially around purpose, to stay grounded, balanced, and capable of staying in the profession in a sustainable manner.

One particular responsibility of educators in America today is to lead the way in promoting anti-racism in our school ecosystems. Anti-racism work is sometimes emphasized exclusively white teachers of students who are Black, Indigenous, or People of Color (BIPOC), and it is indeed vital for educators in predominantly BIPOC learning communities. We are both white women who have spent the majority of our educational careers working with predominantly BIPOC students. We continue to work each day to understand how our white identity impacts our work with students and schools so we can avoid causing more harm to young people and their families. We also want to emphasize that anti-racism work is essential for teachers of white students, because the only way to stop perpetuating white supremacy is by ceasing the indoctrination of all children into systems of white supremacy, and school is where much of that indoctrination happens. This is why we believe the work of reflection is essential and why we continue this work daily.

This book is designed to help you more deeply understand your purpose, including how it is informed by your racial identity. We want to emphasize that we are not anti-racism training experts. This book is not a substitute for doing deep anti-racism work. The suggestions at the end of Chapter 6 can be a starting point for identifying the books, trainings, organizations, experts, and learning communities that can help you do this vital work.

We want to emphasize that we are striving toward anti-racism every day as people and as educators, and we know that sometimes we still miss the mark. We keep trying because we understand the harm done to young people and their communities when educators choose to be ignorant and indifferent about the impact of white supremacy in our schools, classrooms, and society. In her seminal book *Cultivating Genius: An Equity Framework for Culturally and Historically Responsive Literacy*, Gholdy Muhammad writes, "We want to cultivate young people who, across the course of their lifetimes, will disrupt, disquiet, or unhinge oppression." As educators tasked with empowering, inspiring, and supporting those young people, that work starts with all of us in the schools and districts where we teach and lead every day.

Chapter 1

Finding Your Purpose

> "When teachers love their job it shows! The most memorable thing for me about school in general was feeling that sense of support from adults, teachers, and staff at the school. There is nothing more amazing than having at least one teacher who believes in you."
>
> —Martha, Class of 2010

Being an educator is not a job you start when you clock in or walk into your classroom, and it does not end when you clock out or leave the school building. This is why it is so essential to stay connected to your purpose: when things get tough it's hard to walk away for the day or the weekend. Instead, you're more likely to take your challenges home with you and carry them around, leading to the stress and exhaustion that cause burnout. As educators, we need to have a deep understanding of our purpose and what we're passionate about because that's what will keep us motivated to show up for our students and help us keep our fire going day after day.

Your *why* can be your lifeline when you start to feel depleted. Massages and Netflix are temporary, but your *why* is a life source you can return to over and over. In fact, we like to think of reconnecting with our *why* as a way to power up like a video game character that needs more energy. Summoning your sense of purpose can work the same way.

Staying deeply connected to your purpose starts with understanding where it comes from. What life events and people influenced you to become an educator? In our experience, educators sometimes struggle to articulate their true *why*. They can easily explain how and why they entered the teaching profession, but not why they do the work of an educator today. Sometimes they talk about how much they've always loved working with children or mention a teacher who greatly influenced them. Others are passionate about their content or thought that teaching would be a practical use of their degree. These are all important factors in explaining how you entered the profession, but they don't necessarily explain what has kept you going. In this chapter, we share our stories of how we found our purposes as educators, as well as some prompts to help you uncover and connect deeply to your own sense of purpose.

What we reflect on in this chapter:

◆ How Meredith's parents inspired her *why*.

◆ How Rebekah's sense of discord between school and learning inspired her *why*.

◆ Ways to articulate, connect to, and troubleshoot a clear purpose statement.

What we hope you take away from this chapter:

◆ A clear purpose statement about why you're an educator.

◆ How to mine your formative experiences as a learner to understand your purpose.

◆ Especially for leaders: why your school or district needs a purpose, too.

Meredith's Turn

My *Why*, My Drive

From a very young age, I knew I wanted to be an educator. I wanted what I thought was a superpower. I wanted to create a classroom space my students would walk into and know they were going to be supported, loved, and challenged. I wanted to create a space where they could question, grow, and express themselves. I wanted students to love history because it was a class where they would hear and question stories from the past and make connections to today's society. It has always been very important for students to know there is an educator at their school who respects and cares for them as individuals and this is why I became an educator.

As a school leader, my *why* continues to drive me but when I started my journey as an educator I did not think I would be a school leader, such as a principal. I thought I would be a teacher my entire career. What I realized during the later years, as a teacher, is that the true impact I had was what I was in control of and that was the students in my classroom. I realized I wanted to expand my area of influence in the school to impact every student and ensure there was a community of educators who were driven by their purpose. When this shift began to take over my thinking, I knew my purpose was growing and this is why I am driven as a school leader. It was not that my *why* had changed, but I realized how it could drive and push me to lead.

Pain and Loss

I grew up in an upper-middle-class family, where my father was always working and my mother worked only when she wanted to. Both of my parents influenced my decision to become an educator in numerous ways, even though neither were in education. I know my mother was not well throughout the later years of her life and maybe if she was healthy, she might have worked, but her reality prevented her from working. My brother and I were her focus and as she got sicker and could not take care of us, that was what hurt her in so many ways.

My mother was diagnosed with multiple sclerosis when I was seven years old. There were times when she was in remission and there were times when she had flare ups that would lead to her in the hospital, paralyzed on one side, or she would temporarily lose her eyesight. During these flare ups, she never complained about her pain; rather she was always there for her family and friends. I think back on this and think of the strength she mustered to listen to our long-winded stories from her hospital bed. She would smile and just listen. When she was feeling good, she never missed a back-to-school shopping experience, a parent-teacher conference, or a family day. She pushed herself to be present and support us.

I realize that I internalized this strength and drive, which pushed me to ensure I fulfilled my life goal of being an educator. I am inspired each day by my mother's strength to wake up every day in pain and know that her life would end before she met her grandchildren. Her strength lives inside me, lights me up, and gives me strength when I am feeling weak and insecure. As a high schooler, I was given the task at times to take care of my mother. There were times when I had to brush her teeth, comb her hair, change her clothes, and even change and help clean her after she went to the bathroom, but she would look into my eyes and always smile and let me know how she was proud of me and that she loved me. It is her inspiration and strength that lives within me each day to never give up on my goals and desires and this is why I always push myself to be the educator I know I am meant to be.

Becoming Invisible

In high school, I was always a good student who got my work done but I was far from the top of my class. I was the student who completed my homework and studied hard for tests, as learning did not come naturally for me. I had to spend time to ensure I would pass all of my classes. It was always important to me to do well in school even at times when I did not have the energy to get out of bed and perform. I did not want to disappoint my teachers or family. At the same time, during my senior year of high school, I became one of my mother's caretakers along with my father and her loving caretaker Betty. My mom's multiple sclerosis took over her body like a rollercoaster. She became paralyzed, lost her vision, and the day of my high school graduation, she entered into a coma that she never truly came out of.

How did I deal with this sadness and loss? I turned to smoking pot and not taking care of myself. I would go to school most days late and in pajamas. During my lunch break, my friends would ambush me into taking care of myself. I remember on a few occasions going to my best friend Aly's house and she would just hand me a towel and soap and would just tell me she would wait for me after I showered so we could go eat lunch. If I did not shower at her house, I might not have showered for days and I always wore my pj's to school. I also often would go home during lunch and smoke pot before going back to school. Now I know I must have smelled and I looked like a mess and still no one at school spoke to me about this beyond my friends. It was as if I was invisible to my counselors and/or teachers. I was late to school every day and I would go right to the main office and hand in a late note in my handwriting and "signed" by my mom. For the record, my mom could not write as she was paralyzed, so I signed them. I was never called out on it or offered support from my school. These nonactions are what put fire in me to be the educator I became and still strive to be today. I want to ensure that any young person who walks into my classroom or school who experiences pain and loss so deeply knows they are not alone and will never be invisible.

My Drive for Leadership

On the flip side, when I think of my father and his work, I think of a fiercely determined leader who always expressed his company's needs to make sure it was successful. His company, Silver Threads, was one of the first and most successful women's clothing companies for plus-size women. He had a showroom in the garment district of New York City and a factory in New Jersey with over 150 employees. As a child, some of my favorite memories are the days my dad took me into the city to go to work with him. I have vivid memories of driving into the city with my dad and on the way he would take business calls on his car phone (yes, a car phone not a cell phone). During these calls, he would set up for the day. I remember thinking his conversations would get so passionate with his employees and I would think about how it could be hard to work for my dad but in the end this is one of the reasons he was so successful. He believed in his business and he believed that if he was clear with his expectations and goals, then he could ensure his clients would be happy. I also remember when we would get into his office, he would order breakfast and/or lunch for the people who worked for him. He always made sure the company kitchen was stocked and the candy bowl filled for everyone. He also always praised his sales team when they got a new client and his production team knew of their success.

When my dad would come home from work day in and day out, he always made sure my mom had everything he could provide for her to try and reduce her pain and have her live her life to her fullest. I saw his determination to comfort her even when he knew he could not take her pain away. When she lost her ability to climb stairs, he installed electric stairs in our house so she could get from her room to the downstairs and not be trapped upstairs all day. When she could not sleep in their bed anymore, he got her a hospital bed; when she could not get into their car, he got her a handicap-accessible van. He always put every resource he had to try and prolong her life as much as possible.

My father's strength to take care of my mother, continue to run his business, and provide for my brother and me during this time is also integrated into why I am a school leader today. As I watched my father not give up on his business while our family was falling apart, I also saw my father never give up on caring for my mother even when he knew there was nothing he could do to take away her pain. When opportunities came up in my life for me to pursue school leadership, I realized I could have more of an impact and my *why* could expand. I was not only responsible for the students in my classroom but I was responsible for everything that happened at the school. This is when I connected to my dad, and his passion and ability to lead gave me the strength to believe in myself as a school leader. I knew being a leader would put me in situations where I had to have difficult conversations, make very large and impactful decisions, and speak out in a way that challenged my soft-spoken tone. But what I knew is if I put the needs and goals of my students and community first, I could do anything. This drive and passion lived inside me every day as a teacher and continues to drive me as a school leader.

Rebekah's Turn

Schooling vs. Learning

I was an excellent student, probably a dream student for most of my teachers, but I wasn't really in it for the love of learning. I was a perfectionist, terrified of making a mistake, constitutionally averse to failure in any form, and anything less than perfect, or an A, or the best, or number one at anything academic was a failure. School was a place where I excelled, but it was also a minefield where any misstep could mean catastrophe. If I got anything less than a perfect score on a test, my classmates and teachers would ask me what happened. It felt like there was nowhere to go but down.

Learning by reading was a different matter. To say that I loved to read does not come close to my relationship to books. Yes, I read at night when I was supposed to be asleep, but I also read in the car, at the grocery store, in church, at family functions, on the school bus, anywhere I could sneak a book. One day in second grade, I got in trouble for reading *The Secret Garden* in my lap when I was supposed to be listening to my classmates read aloud. (Because my teacher knew my mother, I was terrified I would get in trouble for getting in trouble.) I read anything and everything.

My parents, and especially my grandmother, were the champions of my reading life. My mom would drop me off at Brockway, our community library, to roam the children's section and check out books with my very own library card. I was obsessed with the teen magazines at the library, and eventually my mom bought me subscriptions to *Seventeen, Teen,* and *YM.* When I was in eighth grade, my Aunt Claire gave me a subscription to the holy grail of teen magazines, *Sassy,* where I found book recommendations like *Weetzie Bat, What's Eating Gilbert Grape?,* and Blake Nelson's *Girl,* plus directions on how to turn one of my dad's old dress shirts into a skirt and the admonition that there's no such thing as an abnormal amount of pubic hair.

Because my reading life was separate from my school life, I didn't really think of the reading I did as "learning," even though the discovery of other worlds, cultures, food, lives, places, music, customs, and everything else was what I loved about it. In my mind, reading was different from school. In elementary school, we mostly read from textbooks, and as I got older the books we were assigned bore no resemblance to my actual reading interests—there were no bratty younger sisters, dying ballerinas, or girls getting their first periods, no cheerleaders or high school newspaper editors or football players hanging out at their lockers. It was not until I was in eleventh grade at a public high school for the performing arts that I ever remember even having a choice about what to read for a school assignment: I picked *On the Road* by Jack Kerouac from the teacher-provided list of options. That teacher, Ms. Leone, was a conspicuous exception among my academic teachers in her empowering teaching methods, and one of the most memorable learning experiences of my life was the creative writing lesson where she sent us outside the school building to find something to write about. I wrote about a pickup truck full of cucumbers I saw that day, and I'm fairly certain that story got me into college.

In many ways, my high school was a transformational community where I had formative experiences as a young artist: studying with working professionals in the theater, dance, and music industries; performing in productions with budgets and resources many public high schools could only dream of; and writing plays that were produced for real audiences. It was an incredibly permissive environment where adults entrusted us with creative autonomy and personal independence far beyond what most high school students experience, but it was not a perfect place. As an academically successful white student, the education system was designed to serve and support me, but I did not always feel safe, affirmed, or inspired as a learner there.

In most of my academic classes, we sat in rows, took notes, and studied from textbooks. There was another English teacher who made us copy paragraph-long vocabulary definitions off the board every morning and a math teacher who mocked us as "burger flippers" when we struggled. A ballet teacher kept me after class to tell me I'd be a better dancer if I lost weight, and my guidance counselor tried to discourage me from taking AP Calculus because it might bring down my GPA. After a cast party, I overheard two adult directors joke about raping a student they found attractive, and my history teacher sexually harassed many of us daily, pulling girls onto his lap and once sticking his finger through the button holes of my shirt to touch my skin. And there was a curriculum—both academic and artistic—that lionized the white canon, provoking a protest by Black students a year older than me who interrupted a theater department event to publicly read the names of BIPOC playwrights, composers, and creators whose works we had never studied or performed.

I grew tremendously as a writer and performer there, but I also experienced school as a contested environment where adults could not always be trusted, including with making academic learning something I wanted to do. Instead, it was the battle-ground where I constantly had to prove myself to everyone around me. School was where I did what I was told, took notes because that was what I was supposed to do, and aced tests because failure was not an option. Books and the learning I did outside of school were just for me: reading voraciously and indiscriminately, corresponding with pen pals all over the country, buying albums I read about in zines but could never find on the radio, keeping journals brimming with quotes I'd read or heard, cooking recipes I found in my mom's old cook-books, combing thrift stores for vintage clothes, studying film reviews and event listings in alternative newspapers and then going to the screenings and talks I'd read about.

Finding My *Why*

Years later, when I was a teacher, I started to realize many students were having an experience similar to mine, of school and learning as separate experiences in separate realms, a dichotomy articulated by many scholars including Ivan Illich, Sir Ken Robinson, and Jal Mehta. Like me, my students came to school and were told what to do, how to do it, when to do it, and where to do it. Like me, they rarely made choices about what they read, wrote, or discussed in school. They rarely spoke with passion or curiosity about their schoolwork, but this did not mean there was nothing they were passionate about learning or curious to know. Rather, those were emotions they felt about the learning they did on their own time through activities that were often minimized as hobbies by adults at school: writing poetry, mastering video games, making music, cooking with their families, refining graffiti tags, choreographing dances, silk-screening apparel with their own art, photographing their neighborhoods, reading comic books, creating hair and makeup and nail art, or perfecting their jump shots. They were extremely engaged in the learning they did on their own terms, but this learning felt distinct from what happened at school.

As a teacher, I wanted my students to have the same sense of wonder, possibility, and agency as learners I felt when Ms. Leone sent me and my classmates out into the city to find something to write about. I don't want any students to feel like I did in most of my other high school classes, that school is for someone else and learning is for me. My *why* is to help ensure schools provide all learners—students *and* adults—with access to joyful, vibrant, enchanting, empowering learning experiences that ignite their curiosity and drive them toward even more questions.

Your Turn

Research to Help Excavate Your Purpose

One of our favorite thought leaders on the power of understanding your *why* is Simon Sinek. You can easily find his resources and learn about his book *Start with Why* online, but we recommend starting with his TED Talk, "How Great Leaders Inspire Action." Although Sinek mostly uses examples from business and industry, we think his model for identifying an organizational *why* applies to individuals, too. Sinek's image of the Golden Circle is especially powerful. He says that organizations and leaders often start with "what" they're doing rather than focusing on "why" they're doing it. He makes the case for starting with "why" as a much more effective motivator than "what," and we see a direct application to the work of educators. It is easy to feel overwhelmed and burdened by all the "whats" of this profession, but when you reconnect to your "why" you remember your purpose for doing all of those "whats" in the first place.

Another writer and thinker who has influenced our understanding of purpose is Priya Parker. Like Sinek, Parker is not working specifically in the realm of education. In fact, she's a conflict resolution facilitator, and her book, *The Art of Gathering*, is a powerful argument for changing the way that we come together in community, including in schools and classrooms. From Parker's work, we've learned to use a protocol called The Five Whys. While Parker employs this protocol for uncovering the purpose of a gathering, we have used it for other purposes, too, and we think it's a great tool for understanding your personal *why*. It's pretty simple:

1. Write down your purpose—in this case, your purpose as an educator.

2. Ask yourself why, and write your answer beneath your original purpose.

3. Ask yourself why again, and write that next.

4. Ask yourself why again, and write that next.

5. Ask yourself why again, and write that next.

6. Ask yourself why again, and write that next.

7. Now write your purpose again underneath everything else. Has it changed? Probably! By peeling back the layers of what we think our purpose is, we can get to the true essence of our deepest intentions.

You can find a reproducible version of The Five Whys in the appendix and at https://www.wiley.com/go/educatingpassionpurpose. In addition to using this tool to uncover your individual purpose as an educator, we've used it to articulate the purpose of teams, events, and meetings, including occasions like holiday celebrations. For collective purposes, try having all participants answer The Five Whys on their own and then share their responses with each other to see where there are connections and distinctions. Reflect on what these overlapping and divergent purposes might mean for your community or event.

Excavating Your *Why*

Spend some time journaling or drawing in response to any or all of these prompts to start uncovering your sense of purpose:

- How did you feel about school as a child?
- Who and what are the touchstones of your early experiences in school?
- What was your childhood perception of what a teacher does?

- What role do teaching and learning play in your ancestry and heritage?
- How did your family influence you as a student and/or teacher?
- What sparked your interest in becoming an educator?
- When did you first realize you wanted to be a teacher?
- How did you become an educator?
- Why did you become an educator?
- Why did you stay an educator?
- What is in the soil where the roots of your teaching career took hold?
- If you are not a classroom teacher, how do you think about your role as an educator?

See the Excavating Your *Why* Reflection Tool in the appendix and at https://www.wiley.com/go/educatingpassionpurpose for a reproducible version of this activity. These prompts also work well individually as icebreakers or opening activities at meetings or workshops because they allow educators to get to know each other in new ways. Even though you see your colleagues every day, you might never have spoken with them about these topics, and having these conversations can build relationships and a sense of community around a shared purpose.

Refining Your *Why*

Once you've articulated your why, continue to deepen your understanding of it with any or all of these prompts:

- How has your sense of purpose as an educator evolved?
- Have you ever lost your connection to your *why*? What led to that disconnect?
- How has your *why* changed throughout your time as an educator? What led to this change?

Amplifying Your *Why*

Consider what kinds of reminders will be most helpful to you as you work through this book. How can you turn up the volume on your purpose so that it remains front and center? Here are some suggestions:

- Write your *why* on a Post-it and stick it to your laptop, notebook, or anything else you tend to carry around with you.

- Take a picture of your *why* and use it for the home screen or wallpaper on your phone, computer, or other device.

- Record yourself stating your *why* and use it as your alarm sound.

- Assign a gesture or movement to your *why*. Every time you do it, you'll silently remind yourself of your purpose.

- Write, draw, or use a website like Canva to create a visual representation of your *why* and post it in a place over your desk, on your refrigerator, or somewhere else you'll see it regularly.

- Bonus points: engage your colleagues in articulating their purposes as educators, too, and hang them on a bulletin board in a hallway, office, or staff lounge.

- Double bonus points: engage your students in articulating their purposes as learners and hang theirs and yours in your classroom.

Connecting Your *Why* to Your Work

Consider how your *why* connects to and impacts various aspects of your work. You can jot down notes in a list, a brainstorming web, or any other format that works for you. Here are some ideas to get you started:

- Your students.
- Your school.
- Your classroom.
- Your curriculum (what you teach).
- Your instruction (how you teach).
- Anything else that comes to mind about your work.

Once you've finished making these connections, return to your sense of purpose and explore whether you'd like to adjust it. Ask yourself again: Why are you an educator?

Exploring Your *Ikigai*

Another tool that has influenced us is the Japanese concept of *ikigai*, which Rebekah first learned about through a Bright Morning life coaching course. Your *ikigai* is your purpose, and you find it by seeking the intersection of four key elements:

◆ What you love doing.

◆ What you're good at.

◆ What you can be paid for.

◆ What the world needs.

You can easily find *ikigai* worksheets and graphic organizers online, and we encourage you to explore these resources if this concept interests you, especially if you are considering making a change to your specific role in education more broadly. (More on this in Chapter 6, too!)

Meditating to Discover Your *Why*

We believe meditation can be a very powerful tool to help you connect to and fully understand your purpose. We have both experienced the impact of meditation thanks to the work of Justin Michael Williams. His book, *Stay Woke*, teaches the reader to meditate and makes a case for how it can help us all live the dreams we were born to accomplish. His website, www.justin michaelwilliams.com, has numerous resources for anyone looking to connect to their true purpose. He embodies the idea that this work is for all people of all backgrounds, as everyone deserves to live their life to the fullest.

Personality Tests and Purpose

If you've never taken a personality test, you might consider taking a Myers-Briggs test, an Enneagram assessment, or something similar. These assessments can validate what you already sense about yourself, reveal things you might not be aware of, and point you in possible directions for continued study or exploration with respect to uncovering your purpose and your true mission in life. We encourage educators to take these surveys and consider how their results connect to their work.

The Roots of Your Purpose

To get a deeper understanding of your *why*, reflect on where it came from. Think of the people and events that have shaped your life. How have these individuals inspired you to be an educator and how have these events shaped your beliefs around education? These are the roots holding you up as an educator. Reconnecting to them can help you stay inspired within the profession. The journey of an educator is not a straight road, and there are ups and downs you want to be prepared for. Whether you are celebrating your successes or working to learn from your failures, your connection to the root of your purpose will help push and inspire you to grow.

Troubleshooting Your Purpose

We know from personal experience that identifying, articulating, and committing to your *why* does not always result in smooth sailing. Sometimes this process brings up more questions than answers: What if you can't figure out your *why*? What if your *why* is not inspiring? What if the *why* that used to motivate you no longer resonates? What if your *why* points you toward another profession altogether?

Over the past two decades we've both experienced periods when we struggled with our sense of purpose—finding it, believing in it, and living and working in alignment with it. The most important thing we want to convey here is that it's okay for your purpose to evolve. In fact, that's often a good thing. After all, over time you change, your school changes, your students change, your field of study changes, and the world changes. It makes sense that your *why* might change, too. Finding your purpose is not a one-and-done practice. It's a ritual we have both undertaken periodically and we are still working on. Give yourself permission to approach this process with a sense of curiosity and openness to whatever emerges. This is not a test, and there's no grade for doing it quickly or perfectly.

Your *why* is for you, so take your time and expect the unexpected. As Elena Aguilar writes in her essential book *Onward: Cultivating Emotional Resilience in Educators*:

> Sometimes we might be reluctant to explore our purpose because we fear that we'll uncover a truth that could be hard to accept—that our mission is to travel around the world collecting seeds or to dance on Broadway. If so, explore anyway. It's much better to know what you feel called to do than to wander in a haze. If you

discover that you're in the wrong profession, at least you'll recognize that it's not your principal's fault that you're miserable teaching the new curriculum; it's just that you're being asked to do something that's a total mismatch with why you feel you're on earth.[1] (p. 41)

We talk more in future chapters about how your purpose can help you find the right position—both within and beyond education as well as right down to the specific school level. For now, we want to emphasize that it's better to uncover the truth of your *why*, even if it's painful or scary, than to continue questioning why you're unhappy or unfulfilled or, even worse, blaming your colleagues or your students for how you feel. Sometimes there's a mismatch between what we want and what we have, and excavating your purpose is the first step toward resolving that dissonance.

What If You Can't Figure Out Your Purpose?

Give yourself permission to not have all the answers right away. If you've worked through the prompts and activities in this chapter and still feel unable to articulate your purpose, it might be helpful to step away, continue reading the next chapter, and come back to the question of purpose a little later. If you've been able to articulate a potential purpose statement but aren't sure if it really captures your *why*, give yourself some time to sit with it and see if the resonance deepens. You can always come back to these exercises again.

What If Your Purpose Comes as a Shock?

This might happen. Again, it's okay to have more questions than answers right now. We know that as educators many of us are solution-oriented people who are really good at tackling problems. If your purpose feels like a problem to solve, or it reveals something to you that you were unaware of or didn't want to know, that's good information. Resist the urge to "fix" it and see what it's like to work through the rest of this book with that purpose in mind. You can always come back to the exercises in this chapter later on if you want to try rearticulating your purpose. But maybe your purpose won't feel so shocking if you give yourself some time to sit with it and get to know it a little better. What if you approached your purpose with a sense of curiosity rather than as a problem to solve?

What If Your Purpose Means That Things Need to Change?

That's very possible. Throughout this book, we share examples of changes we've made to bring our personal and professional lives into stronger alignment with our purposes. Sometimes those changes were difficult, scary, inconvenient, or unpleasant. But usually these changes did not have to happen immediately. Once we realized change was necessary, we were able to make a plan and prepare ourselves. Even if your purpose seems like it's going to require you to make changes, it's unlikely you have to make all of those changes right now. So spend some time getting to know your purpose while you work through the rest of this book, and see how you feel about those changes once you've given yourself some time.

What If Your Purpose Changes?

We've both experienced this, and we think it's completely normal. The *why* that brought you into education may not be the same *why* that keeps you going now. You're changing, your school might be changing, the world is definitely changing, so it makes sense that your relationship to your work would change, too.

Additional Considerations for Leaders

Helping Your Community Articulate Their *Why*

As a school leader, it is important to carve out time each year to give your entire staff an opportunity to articulate and connect to why they became educators. The first step in doing this is sharing your own *why* with your community and being very clear with the staff about how your *why* directly connects to your school community. You can start the school year with sharing your purpose or having an activity midyear, and returning to the process periodically throughout the year may also be the right move for your community. You should have your staff sit in a circle without any desks, so everyone is looking at each other during the process. You can have them reflect at the beginning if you think it is helpful, but after you share your *why* with the community, you should open up the space for all to share.

Finding Your Purpose as a Leader

For most school leaders their purpose as an educator in the classroom and as a leader are interconnected, and they might be the same or shift over time. When one becomes a school leader, their locus of control expands to the entire school community. This expansion must also reflect in your *why*. You want to think about how now there are no excuses that an issue within the school community is not something you have a direct impact on or need to address. You should spend time thinking of your purpose and ensure it encompasses this larger goal so you can connect to your *why* when you do not have the energy to solve a problem or the answer for your community. This does not mean you have to always have the answer or the energy but you should always take ownership and work to bring perspective to your community and this begins with your *why*.

Supporting Teachers in Understanding Purpose

At the beginning of the year, school leaders often have individual meetings with their teachers to identify their professional goals. At these meetings, it is important to open by asking your staff what has brought them into the educational field. Why are they educators and why are they at your school? You should have a space to record this, so you can remind staff of their *why* throughout the year in your meetings. We recommend using the Beginning of the Year Teacher Reflection Tool in the appendix and at https://www.wiley.com/go/educatingpassionpurpose. One efficient way to facilitate this for an entire staff is to have community members complete the tool independently and bring it to their meetings with you to discuss, but some educators may prefer to verbally process their responses first and then record their thoughts in writing afterward. This tool also can be used with a partner or coach who asks the prompts and then records what they hear.

Once individual teachers have a clear sense of their purpose, it can be useful also to extend this exercise to the team level. Do your school's teacher teams understand why they exist and have a unified sense of purpose and mission? The resources in this chapter can be used by teams and groups to establish their collective *why*.

Your School's or District's Purpose

Thus far we've focused primarily on our individual sense of purpose as an educator, but schools and districts should have a purpose as a learning community, too. We may use the language of mission, vision, core values, or something else, but the point remains the same: Why does this school exist? What does it bring to its students, families, community, and the world? What is its purpose as a learning institution? Simon Sinek's book, TED Talk, and other resources are great places to start with articulating and developing your institutional vision, which should incorporate voices, input, and feedback from all stakeholders in your community, including students and families. As a leader, you may be the champion of this work, but it should be a collaborative effort.

Asserting an Equity Stance

Assembling a team of stakeholders to safeguard your school or district's commitment to justice and equity starts with writing a mission statement for the team's work. What do you want to focus on? This statement should be inclusive of all members and perspectives of your community. How are you ensuring all voices are incorporated into your mission and vision?

Conduct an equity audit to evaluate your school's or district's practices, policies, procedures, and systems through an equity lens, such as policies around instruction, school culture, grading, dress code, technology use, and other issues. This can be done by an in-house equity team or an outside organization to ensure impartiality. Model courage by publicizing the findings to your learning community, owning the results, and spearheading necessary changes.

Create ways to honor the cultures represented in your community as well as those that are not:

◆ Host ongoing celebrations of cultural traditions (for example, honor indigenous history all year long, not just in October and November).

◆ Embrace and model learning about other cultures.

◆ Advocate around pressing social issues that impact particular cultures and communities.

Be responsive to what's happening in the world and to how different members of your community may react to those events.

Give people what they need, which might not be what they want. For example, BIPOC team members may be triggered or harmed by participating in certain conversations, especially with white colleagues, and may request to opt out. White team members do not necessarily need those accommodations, although they may also request them.

Note

1. Aguilar, Elena, E. (2018). *Onward: Cultivating Emotional Resilience in Educators.* San Francisco: Jossey-Bass, 2018.

Chapter 2

Purpose and Burnout

"A burnt out teacher isn't willing to engage the class with enthusiasm and openness. They always approach teaching as a routine that'll just get them to the end of the day."
—Tevin, Class of 2013

Especially over the past couple of years, burnout has become a catch-all term to describe the malaise educators feel as a result of the pandemic, but it actually has a clinical definition. The Mayo Clinic defines burnout as "a special type of work-related stress—a state of physical or emotional exhaustion that also involves a sense of reduced accomplishment and loss of personal identity."[1] Obviously, teachers experience all kinds of "work-related stress" (anyone who's tried to make copies on an ancient copy machine two minutes before class starts is intimately familiar with at least one type), but burnout refers to something very specific: a sense of having lost your passion, your power, and your purpose.

According to the Mayo Clinic, the following factors contribute to burnout:

◆ A feeling that educators have little or no control over their work, including the decisions that affect their job, their schedule, and access to the resources they need.

◆ A lack of clarity about what's expected of them, such as who's in charge and how they're being evaluated.

◆ A dysfunctional workplace where bullying is tolerated, colleagues undermine each other, or they feel micromanaged.

◆ A loss of equilibrium, where the work feels monotonous or chaotic, and educators constantly have to maintain high energy levels to be productive.

- ◆ A lack of support that leads to isolation, siloing educators in their classrooms or offices with a sense they have to fend for themselves and have no one to turn to.

- ◆ A lack of work-life balance, where educators must spend so much time on their work that they don't have energy for family or friends.[2]

In this chapter, we share our personal stories about burnout, including times when we had to make changes to our personal and/or professional lives to ensure we had the energy to show up every day for our students and school communities. Reading, reflecting, and connecting emotions and actions to purpose can help educators work through burnout and make sure they are on the right path. Many educators feel like they give part of themselves to their students, so when we are in pain or struggling, it can make the profession that much harder. These stories are here to illustrate how we've worked to reflect, prevent, and ultimately overcome burnout.

What we reflect on in this chapter:

- ◆ How leading a school during the COVID-19 pandemic led to burnout for Meredith.

- ◆ How an unexpected change in school leadership led to Rebekah's first experience with burnout.

- ◆ Why recognizing what is and is not in your control is crucial to addressing burnout.

What we hope you take away from this chapter:

- ◆ What burnout is and what it isn't.

- ◆ How to determine if you're experiencing burnout.

- ◆ Why BIPOC educators are especially at risk for burnout.

Meredith's Turn

When Your Work Becomes a Job Rather than a Profession

As an educator, I have always had so many emotions when the beginning of the year rolls around. I am filled with excitement, nerves, and a little bit of worry knowing I have finally settled into summer mode and it is all about to change in just a few days. When September 2020 came around, I had so many emotions that it is hard to describe. That year, I was not as excited as I usually was and I would even go as far as to say that I was already feeling burnt out before it had started. This was the second school year where we were teaching during the COVID-19 pandemic and there were so many unknowns and as the school leader, I knew my staff, students, and families were going to look to me for answers and I did not have many. I did not know if we would be open in person or remote, how long masks would be mandated, if students would be able to log into their Zoom accounts, if the district would provide enough laptops for all my students, and if they did not have WiFi at home how they would connect. I spent the summer planning for every scenario but I did not know if anything would work and if my students would even get an education. This pressure and stress led me to feeling burnout at a time when I knew I could not afford it for my entire community. They needed a strong leader more than ever.

During the pandemic when I was working from home, each day I would wake up and go to my computer and set up for all of my Zoom meetings, phone calls, and spreadsheets. My inability to physically connect to my students and teachers took a large toll on me. Now I am sure everyone in the educational field during this time started questioning their role and purpose.

The year and a half of remote and blended learning tested me in so many ways. It was the pure fact that the purpose of schools were taken from us in many ways. Each day, my teachers would get on their computers and see boxes with letters rather than their students' faces. It felt as if they were talking to themselves and they had little knowledge of how they were doing and if their students understood any of the content they were teaching, and worse that the students were not even thinking while sitting at their computers. The mission and values of the school we worked to help build and create was based on an environment that provides opportunities for students to think critically and question the curriculum they are learning. Through Zoom, there were limited opportunities to do this and it was so difficult to motivate my staff to wake up every day and show up for our students when we could not see them. It was clear that my work became all about trying to predict the future and supporting people without really knowing what I was doing.

My COVID-19 burnout was close to the worst burnout I have experienced but I also learned a lot about myself and the power of being in a physical building with my students and staff. Throughout my life, I always knew I was meant to be an educator but it has been a journey with many ups and some downs. The times I have been down is when I have questioned my purpose and role as an educator, which has led to feelings of burnout.

What Feels Like Burnout but Isn't?

During my first few years in the classroom, I learned quickly that a strong educator must be humble and know they will need support, advice, and time to reflect in order to push themselves through the ups and downs of an educator's life. When I think of those times, during these early years of my career, I do not think they were burnout, because even when I needed to get my mentor to cover my class so I could cry in the bathroom, I knew I needed to learn and grow so I would not cry but rather have the tools and strategies to support my students so they would not push me to a place of tears. The tears came from frustration and defeat, but I got back up and made changes to ensure I could support my students and show them I was not going anywhere.

When I think of burnout, I think of times in my career when I was pushed to rethink my purpose and role within the classroom and/or school. I think of it as a time when my frustrations were so high that I would start to blame others for my frustrations and I started questioning my ability to create a space where students would push their thinking and grow. The times that I am not proud of and they did not feel good. I also knew that when this happened, I was not the educator my students deserved and I needed to take control, reflect, and usually make a change.

Searching for an Identity

The first time I started questioning whether I could continue to be a teacher was in my third year of teaching and my first year in New York City. It was this year where my emotions and feelings ran so high at times that I questioned whether I was burning out on the teaching profession so early or I needed to find a new community or role after the year. Every day, I showed up for my students to teach and I tried my best, but there were times when I would commute to work and I would feel so depressed about the space I was walking into that I would think of turning around. There were even times when I would enter the subway station and wonder if sitting there all day would be better for my mental and physical health than going into the school building. It was those thoughts that made me realize I was getting closer to the emotional drain of burnout and I questioned whether I had the inner strength to pursue my goal within the teaching profession. To me, this was a sign I needed to reevaluate where I was as a teacher and make sure I was not burning out completely.

What Do You Do When All You Do Is Complain?

During my sixth year of teaching, I had the honor of hosting student teachers. This is when I opened up my classroom to an education major who is in their last year of their education program. They get to work with a mentor-teacher to get field experience and work directly with students, while being mentored and supported. This was an amazing opportunity and honor for me, as I had so much respect for my mentor-teacher and I wanted to pass on my passion to new teachers.

So how do I connect this to burnout? I have a distinct memory of mentoring a wonderful student teacher. She had a very strong sense about her from the moment I met her. She was creative, connected, and wanted to dive right into my classroom. I loved being her mentor-teacher, but there were many times when I would find us getting into conversations that would become more like venting sessions than mentoring sessions. I allowed my frustrations with systems and structures at the school to influence my mentoring and professionalism. I knew that as a cooperating teacher I was not supposed to complain. Rather, I was in a position to show an inspiring educator the power of problem-solving and deep commitment to my students and school. These complaining cycles led me to question my role and identity and I knew something needed to change for me to be true to my passion as an educator.

Rebekah's Turn

Shift Happens

On the last day of school in June 2008, we learned that our founding principal, a mentor to me and several of my colleagues, was leaving. Many of us on the faculty were shocked, and not just that he was leaving. Some of us, myself included, were shocked that he hadn't told us privately ahead of time. Maybe that's because he made so many of us feel like he really understood us and valued his relationship with us. But in the end, we felt the same abandonment, betrayal, fear, and loss. I was heartbroken, and it was a terrible end to the school year.

Before his announcement, our principal had already hired a new assistant principal, and that summer a replacement principal was hired, too. Their first school year at the helm was excruciatingly difficult for many of us, including me. Our new principal was well-meaning and kind, but he was unprepared. The assistant principal was also new to the position and had presumably accepted the job with the understanding that he would be working with an experienced principal. When our first principal was there, it always felt like there was an adult in the room, that we would be okay, and he would make sure of it. Without him, the school felt adrift. Losing our principal so unexpectedly, with no succession plan in place, no teacher leadership bench, and only the most tenuous connections to the network and district entities that were meant to support us, left me feeling helpless and unmoored.

My new school leaders and I didn't agree on a lot of things. They seemed like nice guys, but they did not have as much classroom teaching experience as I thought a school leader should have. As an educator who believes a school leader's most important job is to be the instructional leader, it was hard for me to value their expertise.

To be fair, they were thrust into their roles without much support, so they were learning on the job and doing the best they could, and our expectations for them were totally unrealistic because our model of school leadership had been shaped by our previous principal, a man many of us revered. I respected their power and positional authority but was skeptical that I could learn from them. All the burnout ingredients were there, dumped into my own personal pressure cooker. I spent 8 to 10 hours a day working for supervisors I did not have a strong relationship with. I was afraid of the changes they were making and what that might mean for my place in the community and, therefore, the way I saw myself. I felt like no one was in charge, and I was overwhelmed. I felt pressure to take control and responsibility and double down on the leadership roles I'd had in the school for the past four years: leading teams, setting an example about dress code, hiring other teachers, writing curriculum, mentoring other teachers, and so on. All of these pressures pushed me further along the burnout spectrum, and the worst part was that because my administrators had their hands full trying to figure out how to do their own jobs, I was doing it to myself.

Losing My Prep Periods and My Purpose

That year, the idea of "prep periods" was a joke. I ran meetings, organized projects, mentored a first-year colleague, and did a million other things. I got to school at 7:30 every morning and left late every day. I worked all weekend grading papers and planning lessons. There was very little time left for anything else. I was anxious all the time, and I couldn't see a way out, so I also felt hopeless. I knew I needed to do something more or something better, but I had no idea what that was, and there was no one to guide me.

I was trapped in the children's book *Alexander and the Terrible, Horrible, No Good, Very Bad Day*. I said before that I felt like when our first principal left, our school was adrift for a time. We lost our sense of direction. But I also think that was true for me as an individual: I lost my sense of purpose. When I think about that first burnout year and what was driving me forward, I think it was a sense of responsibility to hold things together and try to be the adult in the room who seemed to be missing without him. It was a lot of pressure for one person who had only been teaching for five years.

And yet that wasn't actually my purpose as an educator. I had become completely disconnected from my *why* and was totally consumed by my *what*. I was tearing around like a tornado, all action and dust and noise without anything to ground me in my work. I was doing the things that seemed to need to get done, without thinking about why I was doing them, or what really needed to be done in order for me to further my purpose.

As the 2008–2009 school year drew to a close, I knew I couldn't keep going that way. But I also knew I couldn't control some of the factors that were contributing to my burnout. My school leaders weren't going to change on my timeline, and I didn't want to leave my community or the teaching opportunities I had at my school. I knew I was unhappy and I had a responsibility to myself, my colleagues, and my students to fix how I felt because I was going to make a lot of other people miserable if I didn't.

That was my first burnout year, but not my last. There were two others before I left the classroom for an instructional and leadership coaching position, and two more experiences with burnout happened during the COVID-19 pandemic, once in the summer of 2020 and again in the summer of 2021. In both cases, and this is similar to when I faced burnout as a teacher, I felt trapped. I felt like I had to keep doing something that was making me miserable because I had no choice: people (students, families, colleagues, employees, clients) were counting on me, and I would let them down if I just quit. I had to keep going and deal with all of the changes around me even as I felt powerless to make any changes myself. There was no part of me that wanted to keep doing the work, but I felt like I didn't have the option of saying no. At the same time, I felt like all those things I hated doing were taking me farther and farther away from the work I loved and felt called to do through my purpose.

Your Turn

Identifying Your *Why* Nots

Return to the purpose you articulated at the end of Chapter 1 and reconsider it through these lenses to begin seeing the relationship between your purpose and potential burnout factors:

- ◆ Which aspects of your purpose feel easiest to fulfill?
- ◆ What feels challenging or impossible? Why?
- ◆ What gets in the way of your *why*?
- ◆ Are you too tired for your *why*? If so, what are you spending your energy on instead?
- ◆ Who says "no" to your purpose? (This could include a voice inside your own head.)
- ◆ What's at stake if you don't fulfill your purpose?

Burnout Self-Assessment I

Are you experiencing burnout? Review this burnout checklist adapted from the Mayo Clinic,[3] and mark the questions you answer "yes" to. For every "yes," write down a specific example that captures your experience. For example, if you answered "yes" to the first question, write down something specific you said or thought that captures your cynical or critical feelings about your work. For a reproducible version of this tool, see the Burnout Self-Assessment Checklist in the appendix and at https://www.wiley.com/go/educatingpassionpurpose.

- ◆ Have you become cynical or critical at work?
- ◆ Do you drag yourself to school and have trouble getting started with your day?
- ◆ Have you become irritable or impatient with colleagues, supervisors, students, or families?
- ◆ Do you find yourself blaming your students if they are not meeting your classroom expectations or lack motivation?
- ◆ Do you lack the energy to be consistently productive and engaging with your students?
- ◆ Do you find it hard to concentrate or focus both during and outside of work?
- ◆ Do you lack satisfaction from your achievements as a teacher and from those of your students?
- ◆ Do you feel disillusioned about your work as an educator?
- ◆ Are you using food, drugs, or alcohol to feel better or to simply not feel at all?
- ◆ Have your sleep habits changed?
- ◆ Are you troubled by unexplained headaches, stomach or bowel problems, or other physical complaints?
- ◆ Do you find yourself getting angry at things you can-not control?
- ◆ Have you found yourself doing things at work you could have never imagined in the past?

Burnout Self-Assessment II

As you've read, the Mayo Clinic's definition of burnout is "a state of physical or emotional exhaustion that also involves a sense of reduced accomplishment and loss of personal identity."[4]

- ◆ To what extent does this definition resonate with you?
- ◆ Do you identify with any of these three components: a loss of energy, a loss of power, or a loss of purpose?
- ◆ What are some examples of thoughts or feelings you've experienced that align with each component?

If you determine from this self-assessment or any of the other activities in this chapter that your burnout is caused by lack of time or stress from time management, you can use the Time Management Tool in the appendix or at https://www.wiley.com/go/educatingpassionpurpose to help you create a plan to maximize how you best use your time during the school day. This tool can also be used by administrative and teacher teams to plan how they will use their time to accomplish a collective goal or project.

Using the Burnout Spectrum

In Ernest Hemingway's *The Sun Also Rises*, a character famously describes how he went bankrupt: "Gradually, then suddenly" (p. 141).[5] This is also what we've observed when it comes to teacher burnout. No one wakes up one morning to discover themselves suddenly burnt out with no previous signs or warnings. Instead, the process happens gradually, over time, and then a sudden wake-up call alerts them (or their family, colleagues, or supervisor) to the crisis. We know everyone's experience with burnout is somewhat unique, so we created a Burnout Spectrum to capture what that gradual process can look like. You can find the Burnout Spectrum in the appendix and at https://www.wiley.com/go/educatingpassionpurpose.

◆ Where on the Burnout Spectrum would you place yourself or the teachers you supervise right now? Mark that place on the spectrum.

◆ Do other stages of the Burnout Spectrum resonate with you? Annotate the spectrum to capture your past experiences. You might write a few notes or sketch an image.

◆ Think about the colleagues you know well. Do you see their experiences reflected on the Burnout Spectrum? What have you seen or heard from them that helps you to understand their experience?

Identifying Possible Contributors to Burnout

Review the following burnout risk factors and mark those that resonate with you, either because you have experienced them personally or think the teachers you supervise might be experiencing them:

◆ A feeling that you have little or no control over your work, including the decisions that affect your job, your schedule, and access to the resources you need.

◆ A lack of clarity about what's expected of you, such as who's in charge and how you're being evaluated.

◆ A dysfunctional workplace where bullying is tolerated, colleagues undermine each other, or you feel micromanaged.

◆ A loss of equilibrium, where the work feels monotonous or chaotic, and you constantly have to maintain high energy levels to be productive.

◆ A lack of support that leads to isolation, siloing you in your classroom or office with a sense that you have to fend for yourself and have no one to turn to.

◆ A lack of work-life balance, where you must spend so much time on your work that you don't have energy for family or friends.[6]

Next, complete the following steps to reflect more deeply about what might be at the root of your burnout:

◆ Select the three most significant factors in your experience and write down a memory or story that captures what that experience feels like.

◆ Connect with someone who cares about you and share your story. Ask your partner to simply listen and help you understand your experience without trying to solve the problem or make you feel better. Allow your feelings to be validated. You might discover even more elements of your experience that you want to capture. Feel free to add to your written memory afterward and to repeat this activity with other stories you want to share.

For a reproducible version of this activity, see the Reflection Tool for Burnout Factors in the appendix and at https://www.wiley.com/go/educatingpassionpurpose. When using this tool, it might be tempting to immediately start tackling the factors that contribute to your burnout, but as we recommend elsewhere in this book, give yourself permission to fully understand what the challenges are before you begin identifying solutions. Burnout doesn't have a quick fix and trying to implement one that's unsuccessful might leave you even more exhausted, discouraged, and disillusioned. Instead, work to fully understand the burnout factors that are relevant to you before you start trying to fix them.

Visualizing Your Own Fire

Close your eyes and picture a controlled, purposeful fire, such as a backyard fire pit or a summer campfire. Imagine that this fire represents your professional capacity as an educator. The longer the fire burns, the more effective and enduring your career. If the fire burns too strong and hot, it might become uncontrollable or use up all of the available wood necessary to keep it going long term. If it doesn't burn strongly enough though, it will peter out or not be hot enough to keep you warm. Pull the threads of this metaphor:

◆ If your teaching career is a fire you're trying to maintain, what is the fuel you're burning to do so?

◆ What keeps your fire going?

◆ How long has your fire been burning?

◆ How strong is your flame right now?

◆ Are you using solid, healthy firewood, or twigs and scraps of paper you found lying around?

◆ What happens as your fire burns?

◆ Is there more fuel at the ready, or are you scrambling for something else to keep your fire going?

◆ How do you know when the fire is winding down?

◆ Are you constantly monitoring its state or are you caught off guard when the flame gets low?

◆ Do you want your existing fire to burn continuously or is it necessary to scorch the earth and build a new fire?

◆ What's in the ashes created by your fire?

Allow yourself to sit with this visualization and consider the metaphor from all angles. Notice what rises to the surface for you and feel free to journal about your insights and takeaways.

See the Fire Visualization Tool in the appendix and at https://www.wiley.com/go/educatingpassionpurpose for a reproducible version of this activity. These prompts also work well individually as icebreakers or opening activities at meetings or workshops because they allow educators to get to know each other in new ways. Even though you see your colleagues every day, you might never have spoken with them through the lens of a metaphor like your professional fire, and having these conversations can build relationships and a sense of community around a shared experience.

How Burnout Impacts BIPOC Educators

BIPOC teachers are at even higher risk of burnout than the profession overall. This is because in addition to the burnout factors above that affect all teachers, there are specific factors that BIPOC teachers may also experience:

◆ Micro- and macroaggressions from colleagues, students, leaders, and parents.

◆ The "invisible tax," a term coined by former U.S. Education Secretary John King[7] to describe the increased workload BIPOC teachers are expected to do, such as disciplining or mentoring BIPOC students, translating for multilingual learners, and leading equity work.

◆ Carrying responsibility for preparing BIPOC students for racism they may experience, such as how to "behave" or "code switch" during field trips, internships, and college trips.

◆ Internal pressure to take on leadership roles and additional work because they want students and colleagues to see BIPOC teachers in those roles, provide BIPOC students with role models, and support BIPOC students who may be experiencing struggles they've experienced, too.

How Burnout Impacts Anti-Racist Educators

Anti-racist educators of all races may also experience specific factors that contribute to burnout. We believe all educators should work toward anti-racism, but we also know this is not always the case. When we examine the three components of burnout—loss of energy, loss of power, and loss of identity—through the lens of anti-racism, we can see that educators who are committed to dismantling white supremacy in the education system may be particularly exhausted both physically and mentally by the challenges they face in doing this work. They may also at times feel defeated by the scope of white supremacy and its insidious impact on every aspect of the educational system. And they may begin to question their own racial or professional identity as a member of their school community, particularly if most of their colleagues do not embrace anti-racism. Even if they are committed to justice and anti-racism, they may feel isolated or lose their sense of belonging if other members of their community do not share those commitments. Anti-racism is the right path, but it can be a lonely, stressful, agonizing path that can lead to increased risk for burnout without a sense of solidarity and support. Grounding yourself in your core values, your commitment to anti-racism, and your purpose can help you identify and address what is causing your burnout.

If you're not sure what your core values are, you can find value lists online. We recommend using them for an activity like this one (feel free to adapt the numbers depending on what feels right for you):

1. Circle the 10 values that resonate most strongly with you.

2. Narrow those 10 down to 5.

3. Narrow those five down to three.

Take a step back and review the three values you've selected:

◆ Do these capture what's most important to you?

◆ Are you surprised by any of them?

◆ What do these values say about what matters most to you?

◆ What connections do you see between your purpose and your values?

◆ What might you do, change, or commit to if these are your core values?

You can also complete this activity at an organizational level to identify your school's or district's values.

What If You Think Someone Else Is Experiencing Burnout?

It can be hard to watch someone else struggle with burnout, especially if what they're going through is impacting you as their friend, family member, or colleague. Whether or not you approach them directly about it definitely depends on the nature of your relationship with them, and no matter what, you can't control the choices they make or how they deal with what they're going through. What you can control is yourself, and watching you recommit to your own sense of purpose might help them, too.

What If You Can't Control the Things That Are Burning You Out?

Many things are not within our control, and recognizing that fact is important. But we've also found that many of us have more power than we realize, so it's possible that some of the things that seem beyond your control actually could be affected by your influence, even if you don't have the ability to completely alter them. What you can always control is yourself, and changing your perspective, your response, your understanding, and your approach are often possible. In upcoming chapters, we share examples from our own experiences of how we've confronted burnout factors we could and could not control, and what we've done about them. You'll also find lots of prompts and activities in the "Your Turn" sections to help you engage with these reflective questions on your own.

Additional Considerations for Leaders

As leaders of schools, how do we know when our teachers are burning out? It is essential leaders are aware of the mental state of their educators so they can support them in reflecting and recharging. Leaders need to regularly take the pulse of the stress level in their communities to ensure their students are receiving the best education possible. Following are a few additional prompts that can help leaders.

Is Distributive Leadership Leading to Burnout?

An important aspect of running an effective school is ensuring there is a strong distributive leadership framework influencing and leading systems and structures. At the same time, a leader needs to ensure the distributive leadership is not leading to burnout by overworking the same staff members or by distributing the leader's own burnout to others in the school. The following questions can help leaders assess whether their use of distributive leadership may be inadvertently contributing to staff burnout:

◆ Are the same educators within your community leading all or most initiatives?

◆ As the leader, are you always counting on the same people to take leadership roles? Or do you have a clear structure to develop leadership within members of your community even if they are not fully ready to take on formal leadership responsibilities yet?

◆ When you delegate tasks within your community, are they tasks you do not want to do? Do you fully know how the systems and structures run so you can support your community? Or are you over relying on members of your community to complete tasks you cannot fully support them in?

◆ Are you expecting your teachers to complete leadership roles during their prep periods or do they have time to be leaders as well as plan effectively for their classrooms?

What About Leader Burnout?

As the school leader there is a lot of pressure on you to have all the answers and to be able to control your own emotions in order to ensure the stability and sanity of your entire school community. So how do you know when you are overstressed or burning out as a school leader? School leaders can use the self-assessment resources throughout this chapter, but there are some additional indicators that are unique for school leaders that might mean you are moving down the Burnout Spectrum.

◆ School leaders are often teachers at heart and what gives them joy and motivation are the interactions they have with students each day. When you find you spend the majority of your days inside your office doing paperwork and you do not push yourself to get out from under it, it could mean you do not have control of your time or are losing your personal focus.

◆ To be an effective school leader, you need to see yourself as the lead learner within the community. When you start having moments where you just want your staff to be the experts and you do not want to push yourself to learn all the systems, structures, or new pedagogical approaches to teaching and learning, you need to stop and reflect to ensure this does not lead to burnout. The demands on educators often change in response to local election cycles, and school leaders need to have ways in which they process and grow from this change. But they also need to ensure this change does not take their focus away from their goals as an educator.

Notes

1. Mayo Clinic Staff. (2021). Job burnout: how to spot it and take action. Mayo Clinic (21 June). https://www.mayoclinic.org/healthy-lifestyle/adult-health/in-depth/burnout/art-20046642 (accessed 25 November 2022).
2. Ibid.
3. Ibid.
4. Ibid.
5. Hemingway, E. (1926). *The Sun Also Rises*. New York: Grosset & Dunlap.
6. Mayo Clinic Staff. Job burnout: how to spot it and take action.
7. King, J. (2016). The invisible tax on teachers of color. *The Washington Post* (15 May). https://www.washingtonpost.com/opinions/the-invisible-tax-on-black-teachers/2016/05/15/6b7bea06-16f7-11e6-aa55-670cabef46e0_story.html (accessed 25 November 2022).

Chapter 3

What You Teach

"Teachers that love their job will be fired up
about topics and have an energy about how
they do their lesson that is unmistakable. They
have an aura especially when it is a topic they
want you to learn about very vividly."

—Eli, Class of 2014

As educators, we align our curriculum to state and national
standards, state exams, the mission, vision, and instructional
focus of our school and district, and other factors. Trying to align
curriculum to our own sense of purpose on top of all that might
feel impossible. However, we've found that for teachers to stay
committed to the profession and keep inspiring their students,
they need to ignite their own curiosity and passion about what
they're teaching. This is why we think it's essential for educators
to make connections between their daily work—including
curriculum design—and their personal sense of purpose while
also honoring students' own passions, voices, experiences, and
interests.

Because we know this is a tall order in the face of mandates,
limited time, and other factors that impact curriculum design, in
this chapter we focus on a range of strategies for strengthening
the alignment between your purpose and what you teach. In the
process, we share examples from our own classrooms to illustrate our struggles and successes with finding ways to stay
inspired by and excited about our curriculum. We know the
particulars of our experiences might not be the same as yours,
but we hope you're able to use our examples as sample cases
from which you can glean useful ideas and possibilities, even if
you're working in a different context. The prompts and activities
in the "Your Turn" section will help you ground your thinking in
your specific situation, and we even have some suggestions for

how to keep your fire going if you can't connect to the curriculum you're required to teach.

We also share our experiences with curriculum that was misaligned with our purpose, including preparing students for standardized tests that we did not believe were fair assessments of our students' knowledge and skills and confronting systemic directives we believed were causing harm to our students and to our own mental health. We share what we've learned, what we've done, and what we're still trying to figure out. We also offer some specific guidance for leaders who are responsible for supporting teachers in designing and implementing curriculum, including professional learning and coaching opportunities to strengthen alignment between what teachers teach and why they teach in the first place.

What we reflect on in this chapter:

◆ Some of the lessons that best exemplify how Meredith aligned her curriculum to her purpose.

◆ How Rebekah dealt with the institutional mandates that were not aligned with her purpose.

◆ A few of the questions, writers, and resources that keep us inspired in our work as educators.

What we hope you take away from this chapter:

◆ What it means to design curriculum and teach content in alignment with your purpose.

◆ The potential impact on you and your students when curriculum is misaligned with your purpose.

◆ How to assess alignment between curriculum and purpose and what to do when something feels off.

Meredith's Turn

Bringing My *Why* Out on Day One

When I think of my classroom and the goals I had within my class, I always said I want my students to walk out at the end of the year and say they love history. I was not as concerned with whether they would remember all of the facts I taught them; rather I was focused on whether they would remember the experience of learning, the story of history, and challenging it. Would they remember the debates we had, would they remember the reenactments, would they remember the various scenarios we worked to create new endings to, would they remember the essays they wrote, or the projects they completed? It was very important to me that the content was taught in a way that did not emphasize the skill of memorization. Rather, I wanted my students to walk out thinking like a historian. It was through the structure of the classroom and the specific curriculum I taught that got my students to this place. My role was not to inform my students of the historical facts but rather it was to provide a structure where they could examine the facts and understand how they have impacted the society in which we live. I saw myself more as a storyteller and my students as the creators of meaning and connections.

I did this by opening my school year with a simple picture of the Most Slovenského národného povstania Bridge. I saw this bridge the previous summer when I was traveling through Bratislava. When I saw this bridge, I was fascinated with how it so clearly looked like a UFO and that at the time the top of the bridge was a very expensive bar. Before it was a bar, it was for government officials when Bratislava was in a Communist country. The reason I was told that only government officials were allowed to go into the bridge was because from the top you could see the prospering neighboring country, which was capitalist at the time. So what did I have my students do with this picture on day one? I projected the picture and had my students write a story they thought could be the history of this bridge. Now, because it looked like there was a UFO on top of the bridge, my students would always create extremely creative stories that often involved wars, unique trades, and connections between the two cities this bridge united. My students shared their stories and we discussed how we would know which story is true and if the history we learn is true. We talked about the power of observation and questions. From here, I closed class by telling my students about the actual bridge and its history. I found it essential on day one to ensure my drive as an educator was put into my curriculum. We must empower our students to ask questions and be creative from the moment they walk into the classroom.

Developing Daily Lessons Infused with My *Why*

When teaching about World War I, I wanted my students to understand how the Allies and the Central Powers used trenches in warfare. This led to the creation of a lesson I was famous for. My students were split in two groups and spent the first half of the class designing a battle plan using desk trenches. They planned out how they would place their desks and what their battle plan would be. Then, they had 10 minutes to create trenches and paper balls. They then had a paper ball fight in the classroom. The students then got into a rich discussion critiquing the group's trenches, their war plans, and how dangerous "no man's land" would be to enter. They even applauded or recognized the student who was the bravest soldier, who broke through the trenches first and lost their life for team. This gave students opportunities to connect to the history and ensure there was a role for everyone within the classroom.

When I taught about the Holocaust, we completed numerous activities that helped the students gain an understanding of the different perspectives. One way we did this was reading through a few chapters of a text *Parallel Journey*. This text was about two best friends before the Holocaust; one young boy was German and the other Jewish. They tell their stories about their life as Hitler comes to power and one enters Hilter's youth camps and the other's family goes into hiding and then later a concentration camp. The students would read through these texts, participate in Socratic seminars, and journal. Listening to my students open up and gain different opinions and perspectives when they walked into my classroom was extremely powerful. The classroom was known as a place where you could express yourself, ask questions, and engage with your peers.

I always worked to create opportunities for my students to think critically and I worked to minimize my voice within the classroom. During the Industrial Revolution unit, I split my students into groups and they planned an assembly line that would create a children's book. For students to understand the impact of imperialism, we analyzed the movie *Hotel Rwanda*. My goal within my classroom was that students were not passive learners and their brains were stimulated throughout the period. I always hoped my students questioned the history they were learning and were able to find connections and passion to the curriculum we were studying. This allowed me to build relationships with my students while they built a relationship with history.

When Your Curriculum Leads You to Be Misaligned

Another time when I was teaching and I struggled to connect to the course was when I taught Advanced Placement World History. The sheer amount of curriculum I needed to learn and I needed to ensure my students learned was debilitating for me as an educator. I tried to have my students do the majority of the reading at home so we could engage in discussions while preparing my students for the College Board exam. But I never felt confident in this course and the curriculum. This was a challenging time for me and in the end, I never came up with a solution that felt right. I ended up having a difficult conversation with my administration at the time to change my teaching schedule for the next school year. Without teaching the Advanced Placement curriculum, I was able to focus on my true passion.

Coaching Teachers Using Their *Why*

As a school leader, I love when I have opportunities to help teachers develop their own *why* and support them in creating a curriculum that surrounds and embraces that *why*. There are a few teachers who come to mind when I think of this coaching, support, and development of themselves as an educator and to see a direct impact on their curriculum. At my current school and in my current position, I get to make the majority of the financial decisions for the school. This has allowed me to ensure teachers have the resources and professional development to feed their purpose. We currently are partnered with an outside organization that brings teaching artists into schools to work directly with content teachers to bring complex projects to life. They supported the creation and sustainability of a Maker Space/Fabrication Lab within our school. This partnership has allowed teachers to bring ideas to reality, such as building a model of the Roman Colosseum that students then wrote and directed a play around and used as the main prop, and a full-scale model of a fictitious island and a water dam system, where each civilization that was created explained the benefits and limitations of their geographic features. These challenges, presentations, and experiences continue to spark not only the students within this class but the teacher as well.

I also worked directly with two teachers to integrate social justice issues into the majority of their math projects. I was able to support these educators in finding their true passion and as the school leader secured funding to support these two teachers to attend a professional development out of state that focused on integrating social justice into math curriculum. When they came back and created a unit where students studied the impact of angles, they also analyzed gun control laws and the impact of gun violence on youth. The creation, implementation, and growth of this unit evolved as the teachers were able to continue to develop their passion and were able to see direct growth in their student achievement data. Their students performed at higher rates on standardized exams when they implemented projects that directly aligned to their purpose as educators.

There are so many times I worked with teachers and saw a direct growth in their curriculum when they developed a clear vision for their class and ensured these ideals were aligned in their curriculum. This can be difficult for teachers as they need to ensure they are teaching to standards, meeting the expectations of their curriculum and systems of evaluations for teachers.

Rebekah's Turn

Designing for My *Why*

Is there any better feeling as a teacher than when your students continue a class discussion as they walk out of the room at the end of the period? I sought that every single day. It wasn't enough for my students to be excited about our class when we did special projects or took field trips. I wanted every lesson, every discussion prompt, every vocabulary word even, to spark curiosity and passion. I knew this wasn't actually possible, and certainly not for every student simultaneously, but this was what I always worked toward. I did not yet have the self-awareness or the language to know this was because my purpose as an educator was ensuring my students had access to joyful, vibrant, enchanting, empowering learning experiences. What I knew was that the way I kept my own fire going was by igniting my students' intellectual fires.

What did that look like? I was constantly on the hunt, and I was frequently inspired by a sense of place. For example, during my first visit to the building where I would be a founding faculty member of a brand-new school, my soon-to-be principal took me up to the roof of the five-story building. It was a searing summer day in New York City, and the clear blue sky was punctuated by the high-rises and skyscrapers that surrounded our relatively squat but massive building. Heat waves shimmered above the concrete where faded paint lines marked basketball courts. We shielded our eyes from the blasting sun. My first thought: this would be a great place for Shakespeare.

For the next three years, my ninth grade students read works by Shakespeare in the spring and then performed scenes they designed and directed on that scorching rooftop. We called it "Shakespeare on the Roof." Each year, we held an afternoon performance for the student body, and then an early evening performance for families. One year, a parent approached me afterward to tell me she'd never seen high school students with as much adoration for their teacher as my students had for me. After weeks of coaxing, cajoling, and castigating my students into getting their scenes together, and all of the turmoil that created, of trying to get fourteen-year-olds to memorize Elizabethan English in May when that is the last thing they want to do after a long, cold winter, that parent's comment was a balm I have never forgotten. Many of my students did not like me very much during that preparation process, but when they saw they could really do this thing that had seemed impossible a few weeks earlier, and that other students and their own families were proud of and amazed by and maybe even a little envious of, all of that labor felt well worth it.

Over the next few years, I taught a course for undercredited seniors, and we worked with a teaching artist to create a mural inspired by *The Kite Runner*. I co-taught an elective called New York City Arts and Culture, and every week we took a field trip to a different city site. I designed a summer school class where we read texts set in New York City and then visited those sites, including a day spent riding back and forth on the Staten Island Ferry after reading Edna St. Vincent Millay's "Recuerdo" and a walking tour of Holden Caulfield's Central Park. I scrounged for funding so my students could see the Jean-Michel Basquiat exhibit at the Brooklyn Museum and Broadway shows featuring Denzel Washington as Othello, Jude Law as Hamlet, and Lin-Manuel Miranda a decade before *Hamilton* in his true masterpiece, *In the Heights*. I led an independent study class where students designed their own semester-long projects, including a multimedia photo collection inspired by one student's fascination with lucid dreaming: he interviewed people about their dreams, photographed his own re-creations of them with models, and then set the photographs alongside his own short essays reflecting on his process. That student was well-known in the school for his resistance to traditional classroom methods and his tendency to cut class, but he thrived in that class and later created his own clothing company "We Lurk Late," named for a line in an iconic poem by Gwendolyn Brooks. Another student in that class spent the semester writing an entire poetry anthology of original work. I embraced the intention that my classroom would be a place where students experienced both joy and rigor, that the two were not mutually exclusive.

The Hazards of "High Expectations"

Even though I never really thought about my curriculum through the lens of my sense of purpose, or even knew what my true purpose as an educator was yet, I was steadfast in my belief that every one of my students, regardless of their background or reading level, could do everything that students from more privileged schools and backgrounds could do. I threw down challenges many of my students felt daunted by: reading for an hour a day, learning five new weekly vocabulary words that they would be quizzed on for the rest of the year, writing their own memoir or poetry collection, meditating at the beginning of every class, getting to school early to make sure their paper was on time, reading and understanding and loving *Song of Solomon* and *Their Eyes Were Watching God*, turning an abandoned band room in our school's basement into an interactive haunted house featuring *Jane Eyre* performance art inspired by the immersive theater production *Sleep No More*, bursting into *Twelfth Night* flash mobs in our school's hallways, cafeteria, and even the TKTS triangle in Times Square. These were all things that felt impossible for some or all of my students, but time and again they trusted me when I told them they could do it, and together we did what was necessary to make it happen.

But there was another dimension to my fixation on challenging my students to the fullest extent possible. Throughout most of my teaching career, "high expectations" was a ubiquitous incantation throughout our profession. We heard it over and over and over in meetings and trainings. As an English teacher, I was taught it was the activating motivation behind decisions about what, when, and how students read and wrote and spoke. I learned that young adult literature was fine—great, even—for independent reading, which students were expected to do both in class and at home every day, but whole-class readings were supposed to be "classics" or texts with long legacies or hard-hitting memoirs and nonfiction that captured the world today. I did not yet understand that the traditional literary canon could be used as a weapon of white supremacy culture to exclude other voices and experiences and to reinforce the lie that those voices were not as worthy of being read.

My obsession with "high expectations" wasn't just unhealthy for my students; it was also toxic for me and for my relationships with my colleagues. I took on an inordinate amount of pressure by setting high expectations for myself. "Perfectionism" (another characteristic of white supremacy culture) doesn't begin to describe the way I thought about my work. Every failure felt personal. One of my former colleagues still remembers the day she saw me leaving school with tears streaming down my face. The cause? My students had performed poorly on a practice exam. This obsession with being the best and doing the most created distance between me and my colleagues, and my relationships suffered. I was on the fast track to burnout, and my whole approach to teaching threatened to corrupt the very thing that brought me my sense of purpose. Eventually, I figured out how to ensure that in my classroom "high expectations" actually conveyed my belief in my students and my commitment to designing and facilitating joyful, vibrant, enchanting, empowering learning experiences for them. First, however, I had to reckon with the way I had been trained as an early-career teacher and the unspoken implications of the systemic values (like "high expectations") I was internalizing.

Designing for Transformation

One of the books that has been most influential to me as an educator is not actually an education book at all: *The Art of Gathering* by Priya Parker. This is a book about bringing people together by being a good host, and it transformed my thinking about the role of the teacher. Many educators have heard the platitude about teachers being "the guide on the side, not the sage on the stage." I want to take that metaphor a step further: What if teachers thought of themselves as party hosts? Every day in their classroom they're throwing a party, and their students are their guests. How will they take care of their guests? How will they make sure their guests have a good time and leave thinking, "I can't wait for the next time we get together like this!"? How will they communicate clearly so their guests arrive prepared for whatever the party will entail, wearing the requested attire, potluck dish in hand? Most importantly, how will they ensure their guests feel like this party is the greatest and most important place they could possibly be?

What if we treated time in class with our students like the precious moment in time it is, an hour or less when a group of people come together to be transformed, a period of time that will never come again? As Tom Wayman writes in one of my favorite poems about teaching and learning, "Did I Miss Anything?":

> Contained in this classroom
> is a microcosm of human existence
> assembled for you to query and examine and ponder[1]

A question I love to ask teachers I'm coaching is, "How will students be different at the end of this lesson than they were when they walked in the door?" Students come to class to learn, and learning is a transformative process. So, what transformation will students experience as a result of their time in class today? When we don't think of our classrooms as transformational spaces, much of what happens there can feel stiflingly transactional. So, what if instead we thought about classrooms as places where great change happens every single day, assemblages of humans brought together to question and explore and dream, where on any given Thursday at 10:06 in the morning, a young person will suddenly see something in a new way that will change the course of their life?

The beautiful thing about being an educator is that every fall we get to begin again. We get to welcome a new community of students, and we can be and do better for them. This was true for me as a classroom teacher and even more true once I began to work with adults as a professional learning designer and facilitator. During our final year as classroom teachers, Meredith and I served as teacher leaders, and we took on the task of designing and leading professional learning for the entire faculty every Wednesday afternoon, doing our best to improve upon the decade of boring, admin-led, sit-and-get professional development sessions we'd had to sit through ourselves. The sessions I'm proudest of are the ones where we recruited students to teach their own teachers. Now that I have my own company with even more autonomy in how I design and facilitate educator workshops, I seek out opportunities to host events that bring teachers and students together to build intergenerational learning communities that deconstruct traditional hierarchies and methods. Even though I have many regrets about what I expected my own students to read and learn, I also keep trying to do better for the learners I have the privilege of working with now. Your *why* doesn't have an expiration date, and it's never too late to recommit to it.

Your Turn

Assessing Your Curriculum

Return to the purpose you articulated at the end of Chapter 1 and reconsider it through these lenses:

◆ What does your purpose mean for what you teach?

◆ If the content of your course is aligned to your purpose, what will your students be learning?

◆ What are important aspects of your curriculum that further your purpose?

◆ Where have you already been successful with teaching in alignment with your purpose?

◆ What barriers have gotten in the way of teaching in alignment with your purpose?

Once you have examined your purpose, you can review your curriculum and identify places where your curriculum directly connects to your passion. What do you love and why? Why does it inspire you? When you have a deep understanding of this connection between your curriculum and your sense of purpose, you can start planning how to replicate it. For additional ideas on how to align your curriculum with your purpose, check out the Purposeful Planning Tool for Units and Lessons tool in the appendix and at https://www.wiley.com/go/educatingpassionpurpose. It's designed to accompany your existing planning tools and can be used by teams, co-teachers, or other professional learning communities that plan collaboratively.

Analyzing the Lessons That Resonate

Many teachers have favorite lessons, the ones they remember years later and that their former students remember, too. These are the lessons teachers look forward to and future students may have already heard about. Choose one of your favorite lessons and consider:

◆ Why does this lesson resonate so strongly with you and your students?

◆ What content and skills do students learn through this lesson?

◆ How does this lesson connect to your purpose?

◆ What can this lesson teach you about what keeps you inspired and energized about your work?

What If You Hate Your Curriculum?

Sometimes teachers can't control what they teach and find themselves planning lessons that don't excite them. We know many educators teach curriculum that is mandated at the state, district, or school level, or that has been collaboratively designed by a team where individual adjustments aren't possible. How do you teach a curriculum that does not inspire you? Is there a way to reconsider your preconceived notions about what you're teaching and find inspiration by focusing on the needs of your students? What other changes can you make to help you live and work in stronger alignment with your purpose? Here are a few tips:

◆ Take some time to read through the curriculum and highlight the content that most interests you.

◆ If you have flexibility with sequencing, start with the unit that excites you the most.

◆ Think about your pedagogy: Can you teach this curriculum in a way that is aligned with your *why*? For example, if your curriculum centers on white voices and experiences, can you teach your students to critique those perspectives and this curricular bias, rather than reinforcing them?

◆ Create a personal bibliography of the writers and thinkers who inspire you, or a journal where you record quotes and ideas that resonate with you. Schedule time to read, write, and reflect on the words that make you feel inspired and empowered.

◆ Don't give up. Keep looking for opportunities to connect to your curriculum in ways that are personal and meaningful for you and your students.

◆ Think about what is in your locus of control. If you can't change your curriculum, what *can* you change?

◆ Use the Modifying for Misalignment Tool in the appendix or at https://www.wiley.com/go/educatingpassion purpose to help realign a unit or lesson with your purpose.

Standardized Tests Aren't Everything . . . But They Are Something

Another unavoidable feature of the educational landscape many educators feel beholden to are the standardized assessments their students must take. For many students, these tests have significant, even lifelong implications, and teachers are often evaluated or judged by their students' results. This is why having a clear sense of your purpose is so important. It's unlikely you became a teacher because you wanted to help students do well on standardized tests. But let's say your purpose is to empower young people to achieve their dreams. This requires an expansive sense of possibility: your students must have as many pathways available to them as possible so they can get wherever they want to go in life. Unfortunately, standardized assessments often serve as gatekeepers along certain pathways. So for you to teach in alignment with your purpose, you're going to need to teach your students to identify, prepare for, and open those gates for themselves. They will not be served by a lack of preparation for standardized tests or a sense of helplessness about their ability to succeed on them. Instead of "teaching to the test," you may find you need to "teach the test" so your students understand how the test works, what it's supposed to measure, and whose interests it was designed to serve. Once you have armed your students with this knowledge, they will be better equipped to tackle these gatekeepers, and you will be helping them to achieve their dreams by understanding how to combat some of the obstacles that might get in their way.

What If You're Still Learning Your Curriculum?

First of all, good for you for embracing a learner stance about
what you teach! We don't recommend trying to change your
curriculum if you don't feel like you completely understand it
yet. Once you've taught your curriculum and have a better sense
of how you and your students are engaging with it, you can start
to think about the relationship between your curriculum and
your purpose.

Additional Considerations for Leaders

Professional Development

As a leader, you can create an environment where teachers are
empowered to create and teach curriculum aligned to their
purpose by ensuring teachers have a voice about the professional
development experiences your school offers. This involvement
helps them connect to their curriculum and the school's instructional focus. It's a key area where teachers need to be at the
center of your school's decision-making process.

A few questions leaders should use to evaluate their professional development include:

◆ Who plans the professional development in your school?

◆ What role do your teachers have in the creation of professional development?

◆ How often do teachers get to reflect and give feedback
about professional development?

◆ How do you incorporate teacher feedback into professional development?

◆ How often do teachers take time to reflect on their curriculum and connect it to their goals and purpose?

Curriculum Design and Support

When it comes to curriculum planning, it is essential teachers
take time to evaluate the content, skills, and material they teach
through the lens of their purpose. If your school uses required or
suggested curriculum planning templates, assess the extent to
which they prompt teachers to consider purpose during the
planning process:

◆ Do your school's curriculum design materials support teachers in thinking about their purpose while they are planning for the year, unit, or lesson?

◆ Do teachers have opportunities to plan, offer feedback, review student work, and revise plans together?

◆ Do they regularly self-assess whether or not they are teaching in alignment with their purpose?

◆ How do you support teachers in "teaching the test" without teaching *to* the test?

◆ How do you empower teachers to question their preconceived notions about curriculum?

◆ How do you support and challenge teachers who resist the curriculum?

◆ What kind of flexibility can you offer teachers in curriculum design? How can you make space for them to be creative and inspired no matter what they teach?

Note

1. Wayman, T. (1993). "Did I Miss Anything?" *Did I Miss Anything? Selected Poems 1973–1993*. Madeira Park, British Columbia: Harbour Publishing. https://www.loc.gov/programs/poetry-and-literature/poet-laureate/poet-laureate-projects/poetry-180/all-poems/item/poetry-180-013/did-i-miss-anything/ (accessed 25 November 2022).

Chapter 4

How You Teach

> "I know my teacher is burnt out when they
> don't seem happy when in a class and teaching.
> They don't give us the information that we need
> and turn to independent work every day. It
> makes the classroom very tense and
> uncomfortable."
>
> —Emmy, Class of 2026

In the previous chapter, we talked about curriculum: what you teach. In this chapter, we focus on instruction: how you teach. Your instructional methods are the strategies, techniques, and practices you use to engage students with the curriculum. We are not promoting any particular instructional models or techniques here. Rather, our focus is on examining the relationship between how you approach your work and the potential for burnout. We believe it's essential to recognize what you're doing, how it's affecting you and your students, and what you can do to change any approaches that aren't serving you, your passion and purpose, or your students.

The instructional methods you employ in your classroom should be aligned with your purpose. You of course need to honor school and district policies, but it is also important to think about your own beliefs and their relationship to these policies to make sure you are able to implement them consistently, authentically, and with integrity. Your instructional methods frame your daily interactions with your students, so ensuring they're purpose-aligned is key to keeping your fire going. As in the previous chapter, we share examples from our own teaching and leadership experiences to illustrate how our beliefs about instruction have evolved over time as we've gained a deeper understanding of our purpose. These shifts in our thinking have often been in response to what was happening in the world around us as we witnessed the impact of those events on the young people we work with.

We know the specifics of our experiences may not resonate with all readers, but we hope that our struggles and successes with classroom management, reading instruction, and other elements of our teaching practice ground the reflective practices we're sharing in real-world examples. You'll find prompts and activities to support your own reflection on purpose and instruction in the "Your Turn" section, including ways to root your reflective work in the practice of listening to yourself and your students.

What we reflect on in this chapter:

◆ How we internalized and wrestled with the advice of mentors and professors as early-career teachers.

◆ How we came to understand the impact of systemic forces in our own classrooms.

◆ How our teaching methods changed over time as we developed a stronger awareness of purpose.

What we hope you take away from this chapter:

◆ What it means to develop and implement instructional methods in alignment with your purpose.

◆ The potential impact on you and your students when your teaching practices are misaligned with your purpose.

◆ How to assess alignment between instruction and purpose and what to do when something feels off.

Meredith's Turn

Gaining Respect and Building Authentic Relationships

The most important aspect of my classroom was the time I spent building relationships with my students. One piece of advice given to me by a colleague that impacted me was to ensure I take my ego out of my work. This is a mantra I try to hold onto on a daily basis. When my students said negative things about my class or did not focus in class, it was hard for me to not take it personally. But I realized it was not because students did not like me that they would get distracted. Rather, it was when I did not explain my expectations to students or when they did not see the purpose of the learning that they would not want to complete the work.

I also learned that part of building the relationships with my students was recognizing the impact my race has on my life. When I met with students individually, I talked about how being a white woman impacts my life and my decisions in a different way than their race impacts their life and their decisions. This openness and acknowledgment brought me closer to my students and led to many rich conversations. When a student came in late to class, I talked to them to find out what prevented them from coming on time. When a student was disinterested and fell asleep in class, I didn't see that as them rejecting the class, but as a moment where I needed to stop and talk to the student at a different time of the day to find out how I could best support them. When a student showed signs of being in crisis, I brought them to a counselor to get help. It was very important to me that my students knew that I was there for them, to learn about them, and support them. This had a direct impact on how I taught each and every one of my lessons.

Systems and Structures That Empower

I believe students misbehave in a classroom when they do not know the expectations of the classroom and when they do not understand the content or cannot access it. This is why I think classroom management issues stem from instructional and/or pedagogical issues in the classroom. This, of course, took time for me to develop and I have numerous stories where I raised my voice or took class points away from students to attempt to get them to follow classroom expectations. As well, there are plenty of times where I did not know what to do. But throughout my years, I discovered the most important thing was to try to align the systems and structures in my classroom to empowerment.

One very important way was through ensuring my students knew and believed in my class motto. In the front of the room, I had a huge sign in large writing that read, MAKE AN EFFORT, NOT AN EXCUSE. I told my students every day, the most important thing in this classroom is your effort. You must try to grapple with the history we are studying, you must ask questions, you must express your thinking whether it was verbally or written. And your effort within the process was more important than getting the correct answer. This motto ended up transforming not only the culture of my classroom, but the way I structured my lessons, my homework, and grading policies. It became the thing I was known for as a teacher. Students would say that if you tried and put your thinking forward in Ms. Parmett/ Ms. Matson's class, then you would be supported and encouraged to succeed. This might seem like a small step, but the consistency and dedication I had toward this model reduced some of my own inner stress within the classroom that could lead to frustration, burnout, and stress. I lived by this motto and I helped my students embrace it.

The First Five Minutes of Class Are the Most Important

One thing one of my mentor teachers told me during my first year of teaching is that the first five minutes of a class can determine the entire period. Now, at first I thought of this from a behavioral point of view. If I can "control" the class for the first five minutes, then I can "control" them for the entire period. I would say things like, "Remember when everyone was focused during the Do Now? This is what I expect now." This silent, working tone can then continue the entire period. But as I grew as an educator, I understood what my mentor was showing me. If within the first five minutes of the class you have every single student thinking, questioning, and interested in the learning, they will stay with you for the entire period. This is why it was so important to me to have a classroom that started from the beginning where all students, no matter what, could access the material with absolutely no excuses. Thus, for the rest of the class, students would know the expectation in this classroom is that we will think deeply for the entire period. This routine was so important to my class because it showed every one of my students that there is not a barrier to learning within my classes. We must be prepared to activate our brains and get our minds on and ready to question and engage in the curriculum.

Take Control of Planning

My first two years of teaching, I taught in rural North Carolina and lived with three other teachers in a four-bedroom house and all the people who I saw throughout my days were other teachers. There were very few things that distracted me from spending most of my time planning for my classes. I will never forget a few times staying at school until about 8 p.m. The other seventh grade social studies teacher and I stayed in our classrooms to plan for our upcoming lessons. When the custodial staff came by to do their classroom checks, we hid or let them know we were leaving. Then when we were ready to leave, we called each other and we climbed out of our windows to leave the school, as the building was already locked up for the night. The other teacher had a pickup truck and he literally picked me up after I jumped out of my classroom window. Now, I know this sounds so crazy, but living with all teachers in a small town, we spent a lot of time thinking and talking about our classrooms. I always strove to find new ways to connect to my students and I knew I needed to be prepared and planned for the upcoming day, as I needed to be ready when my students showed up. As an early-career teacher, I learned firsthand that you cannot put every waking moment into planning for your classroom because for my first two years there were many days that I felt like this is what I did. As I moved from teaching in rural North Carolina to New York City, I knew something had to change for me to continue my life goal of teaching.

How did I change these practices and take control of the necessary planning that goes into teaching a strong lesson each day and ensure I was servicing all my students without burning myself out? There are a few things I discovered over the years that helped me. The first is I came to terms with the fact that I did not need to be the expert in all the history I taught. With that being said, I was very up front with my students that there would be times when they asked me questions and I would not have the answers and that there would be times when I was learning along with them. Sometimes, I had to answer their questions the next day or I would challenge the student and myself to come back with an answer. Alleviating this pressure to know everything helped me get deeper in my planning rather than letting this stifle me.

Another thing that helped me was recognizing that every day I did not need to change my pedagogical approach to my classroom. I developed a very strong structure in my classroom and each day I stuck to that structure and then allowed myself to be creative within that space. This meant that every day my class started with a 5 to 10 minute "do now" opener, then I taught new material on the specific topic for the day—this could be a lecture or a reading for students—and then the bulk of the class was a student-centered activity that allowed the class to apply the concepts they were learning for the day. Finally, there was a clear closing activity. These activities were where the class came alive. We held debates, Socratic seminars, student-created projects. The closing activity became extremely standardized by the end of my teaching career. I had students complete an "analyze that" activity at the end of each class. Students had to reflect on the learning target for the day and analyze it. They had to prove they understood the main concept and then a few students would share their responses and students self-assessed their answers.

Within this structure I found creativity but also a sense of stability, which allowed myself to control the planning process rather than feeling like the planning was taking over my life. It also brought stability to my students. They expected a structure when they walked into my classroom even if they did not always know where it would take them.

Rebekah's Turn

Keeping My Students' Reading Fires Going

When I first entered the teaching profession, I was indoctrinated into a system that teaches white educators in urban communities to be afraid of their students, to see their students as always potentially out of control if not for disciplinary policies and strict classroom management. As a new teacher, I was afraid of my students and of losing control of my classroom. Where did this fear come from? No one ever directly told me to be afraid; it was coded. My teacher preparation trainers and professors told us that "these kids"—our Bronx students, most of them Black and Latinx—would only respond to strict discipline. *Be tenacious with your routines. If you fail to plan, plan to fail. Don't smile before Thanksgiving.* I absorbed every stereotype, every coded message, every racist belief without thinking twice or questioning where those messages came from and who they served. I did not even think to object to the joyless, antiquated curriculum my department leader handed me that first semester even though the books were entirely by white authors, all but one of them men. I accepted that this was what I was supposed to be teaching, and I did not want to rock the boat.

For the first half of my teaching career, I was oblivious to the disconnect between my experiences as a young reader and how I ran my own classroom of young readers. I could not see that I also was creating a dichotomy between schooling and learning for my students by running a teacher-centered classroom, including choosing the books we read and insisting that we all read those books together at the same time. Not only was I ignorant about the harm I was doing to my students' engagement in reading, development of a reading identity, and sense of themselves as empowered learners, but I also was creating a tremendous amount of additional work for myself that contributed to burnout risk. For starters, I had to spend every summer reading and rereading the books I would teach the following school year instead of being rejuvenated by what I really wanted to read on my own time. I spent most weekends planning lessons when I wasn't grading papers. Worst of all, I felt frustrated and disheartened when students didn't love the books I had chosen, selections that were generally determined by my own reading interests and passions, not my students'. At best, most of my students seemed to read these books because they had to, not because they wanted to. At worst, they didn't read them at all. As someone with an unbridled passion for reading, it was soul crushing to see my students merely tolerating books.

I was suffering, but more importantly, so were my students. As a white woman leading classrooms of Black and Latinx students, mostly young men, I was reinforcing racist structures that concentrated power, authority, and expertise in the hands of a single person with positional authority in the classroom and even more institutional power at the ready to back me up.

As I became a more experienced teacher, I learned more about the broader educational landscape, and my philosophy of education changed. By visiting other schools, becoming an adjunct instructor at a graduate school of education, meeting teachers from other schools and districts, and becoming an Advanced Placement exam scorer, I learned more about what teaching and learning looked like outside the bubble of my school, including approaches that empower students through voice, choice, and agency. I realized that "high expectations" didn't mean reading the canon or achieving the best test scores; it meant empowering students with ownership of their learning. I started to understand that the purpose of my classroom was not to teach young people how to fall in line; it was to teach them how to see the lines and then redraw them.

I knew from my own experience as a student that many middle-class white students were not subjected to the school and classroom conditions that my students were, and I knew I did not have control over many things that my students experienced, but I seized the opportunity to change what I could control. I started with my bathroom policy: students no longer had to ask permission to use the restroom. More significantly, I made lots of changes to my curriculum and instruction including changes to the books my students read, my grading and assessment policies, and the kinds of projects I assigned. I was taking steps to empower my students by revamping my curriculum and shifting my instructional approach. I started volunteering to teach electives where I could experiment with independent study, field trips, arts integration, and experiential learning. I started to see my students' freedom—both within and beyond my classroom—as my guiding objective, not fear.

I began experimenting with more student-centered methods of text selection, reading communities, and independent reading to ensure my students were always reading at least one book of their choice. For one project, I matched up my students with other educators at our school—not necessarily classroom teachers—as reading buddies. I had my students select a book they wanted to read independently, and then sent the entire list out to my colleagues. Staff members who wanted to participate signed up for a book on the list they were interested in reading, and then met with the student who had selected that book for reading conversations my students prepared and facilitated. Those were high expectations, regardless of what book my students chose.

These instructional approaches meant I could no longer be an expert on everything my students read but also that I didn't need to be because there were other members of the community who served as their learning partners, including their peers and other educators at my school. By shifting more of the responsibility for learning onto my students, I took the pressure off of myself and cultivated a more authentic reading and discussion experience for them. The fact that I brought other members of the school community into my classroom as reading teachers, regardless of their actual job title, provided my students with models of how adults actually read when they don't have to but rather choose to. By honoring student voice and choice, I allowed my students to develop a reading identity and sense of themselves as readers by cultivating habits that hopefully would lead to lifelong reading. I also fostered in my students a sense of the world as text, not just the "classic" books often written by dead white men that so often form the foundation of an academic reading list. Instead of planning curriculum (what to "teach" about this book), I could focus almost exclusively on instruction (how to engage my students in thinking deeply about literature and then effectively expressing those thoughts through discussion and writing). I empowered my students to make their own choices about what they read, including texts I never would have chosen or even known about.

Most importantly, I was teaching in a way that was more closely aligned with my sense of purpose in ensuring all learners have access to joyful, vibrant, enchanting, empowering learning experiences. What is more joyful or enchanting than falling in love with a book? Getting to read what they wanted and taking responsibility for their learning were empowering experiences for students. Doing so allowed us to make the curriculum and the classroom a collaborative endeavor between me and my students because we were building the learning environment together. By reimagining what teaching, learning, and grading could look like in my classroom, I was moving closer to an equitable learning environment with students at the center, where young people decided what to read, how to talk about it, and when they were satisfied with their work. I came to understand the difference between "high expectations" based on goals adults (whether individually or institutionally) set for students and those students commit to for themselves.

Reframing Resistance

Then, on the night of Saturday, March 9, 2013, a tenth grader at our school named Kimani Gray was killed by the NYPD in Brooklyn. Four months later, George Zimmerman was acquitted of murdering Trayvon Martin, and the film *Fruitvale Station* was released, reigniting outrage about the 2009 killing of Oscar Grant III. Kimani's name appeared on signs and T-shirts at Black Lives Matter protests against police brutality and the murders of Black men and women by law enforcement officers throughout that summer and fall and into 2014 when Eric Garner was killed, also by the NYPD. I read Ta-Nehisi Coates's 2015 book, *Between the World and Me*, and this sentence about his educational experience stopped me in my tracks: "The classroom was a jail of other people's interests" (p. 48).[1] Was that how my students experienced my classroom, as a jail of other people's interests, including my own?

It was during this period that I left my job as a classroom teacher to become an instructional and teacher leadership coach at schools across New York City. Now I was sitting in classrooms, not standing at the front of them. For the first time after a decade in public education, I spent most of my days looking at classrooms from a student's perspective, and it was thoroughly depressing. It was boring. It was uncomfortable. I deeply identified with the students who put their heads down on their desks or were preoccupied with their phones. I was on my phone, too; napping and checking my email often seemed like a far better use of my time. Tasks were often boring, simple, nonsensical, pointless. I had always received tons of positive feedback about my teaching, with colleagues who wanted to learn from me and alumni who returned to tell me how much my class had prepared them for college, but now I started to rethink everything I thought I knew about my instructional expertise. I realized it was entirely possible—likely, even inevitable—my own classroom had been marked by the same colossal wasting of young people's time. Yes, I had made changes in my classroom with the goals of empowerment and expression. But now I saw how much more I needed to do.

Students in the classrooms I observed were often considered "behavior problems," and it started occurring to me that at least some of their actions were resistance to injustice. The students I taught and observed understood that dress codes, grades that reward compliance, inhumane bathroom policies and conditions, curricula that ignore or reduce the contributions of Black, Indigenous, and people of color, inequitable school facilities and opportunities, racial and socioeconomic segregation, and hiring practices that result in schools with mostly BIPOC students staffed by mostly white teachers and leaders are all a reflection of systemic forces. They often understand this dynamic even better than the staff members who design and enforce these policies, the very policies they themselves were trained to subscribe to, as I was.

I came to understand that for many students, school is a fundamentally disempowering experience. They find themselves with very little control over anything, from what they read to how fast they need to learn to what they wear to when they eat to whether or not they can use the bathroom. But what they do retain control over is their voice, and for many students this is how they register their resistance. They were pushing back against the systemic forces writ small in my classroom by my own complicity. Essentially, these students were demanding higher expectations of me. My students had achieved high levels academically, but at what cost? What harm had been done? And what might have been different if I had been able to apply an understanding of racial justice to my instruction?

I have worked with many educators who had the strength to keep teaching through unconscionable loss and struggle. Colleagues in losing battles with cancer, who suffered miscarriages, watched a grown child die, or went through divorce. An entire staff that showed up in every way they could the Monday after Kimani was killed. I know how hard teachers work, and I wholeheartedly believe the vast majority of teachers are doing their best. But the transformation that becoming a coach sparked in me was the understanding that students need us to do way better. The work of dismantling white supremacy in our education system and in ourselves never ends, and it's not separate from our work as teachers and leaders. It is the work.

Your Turn

Assess Your Instruction

Return to the purpose you articulated at the end of Chapter 1 and reconsider it through these lenses:

◆ What does your purpose mean for how you teach?

◆ If your instructional methods are aligned to your purpose, how will students be learning?

◆ What are important aspects of your classroom environment that promote your purpose?

◆ Where have you already been successful with teaching in alignment with your purpose?

◆ What barriers have gotten in the way of teaching in alignment with your purpose?

Next, review your instructional practices and identify places where your methods directly connect to your passion:

◆ What do you love about helping your students learn and why?

◆ How does student learning inspire you?

When you have a deep understanding of this connection between your instruction and your sense of purpose, you can start planning how to replicate it.

What If You Have to Use Mandated Instructional Methods?

Sometimes teachers can't control how they teach or the policies that frame their instruction. Consequently, they find themselves creating a learning environment that doesn't excite them or might even be in conflict with their own values and beliefs. How do you teach in an environment that does not inspire you? Is there a way to reconsider your preconceived notions about how you're teaching and find inspiration by focusing on the needs of your students? Here are a few ways to mitigate this misalignment:

◆ Take some time to review the research supporting any instructional mandates or policies for your school or district and highlight the findings that most interest you.

◆ If you have flexibility with your curriculum, focus on the content that excites you and your students the most.

◆ Think about the intersections between your curriculum and your pedagogy: If your school requires you to assign written homework every night, can you design authentic tasks that are more relevant, enjoyable, and manageable for you and your students? For example, instead of assigning the questions at the end of a textbook chapter, can students create a newspaper headline, social media post, or meme summing up the most important content?

◆ Create a personal bibliography of the writers and thinkers who inspire you, or a journal where you record quotes and ideas that resonate with you. Schedule time to read, write, and reflect on the words that inspire and empower you.

◆ If you don't have one yet, adopt a classroom motto to inspire you and your students in alignment with your purpose, and post it somewhere visible so you can all see and refer to it regularly. In this chapter, Meredith explains how she used "Make an effort, not an excuse." Here are a few that Rebekah used in her classroom:

- ◆ "What you pay attention to will thrive."

- ◆ "Insanity is doing the same thing over and over again expecting different results."

- ◆ "You think your pain and your heartbreak are unprecedented in the history of the world, but then you read." – James Baldwin[2]

◆ Don't give up. Keep looking for opportunities to enhance the learning environment in ways that are personal and meaningful for you and your students.

◆ Think about what is in your locus of control. If you can't change a specific mandate or policy, what *can* you change?

◆ Use the Connecting Schoolwide Policies to Your Purpose tool in the appendix and at https://www.wiley.com/go/educatingpassionpurpose to help you plan how you'll implement institutional policies with authenticity, integrity, and consistency. (This tool can also be used to connect schoolwide policies to a school's own purpose.)

Listening to Your Students

If we listen to our students, they will tell us what they need. Implement regular opportunities for your students to provide you with feedback on how things are going in your classroom, such as through an anonymous written or digital survey, a town hall-style discussion, or focus groups. See the Sample Student Feedback Survey in the appendix and at https://www.wiley.com/go/educatingpassionpurpose for an example of a student feedback survey Rebekah administered to her students.

Your feedback questions might include age-appropriate versions of the following:

◆ What's working for you?

◆ What do you wish was different about this class?

◆ What's the most exciting learning experience you've had in this class this year?

◆ What would you like to do more or less of?

◆ Where do you feel you have a voice in this classroom?

◆ Where do you feel you've been silenced by classroom, school, or district policies?

◆ If you could wave a magic wand, what would you change about your learning experience?

Once you've reviewed your students' feedback, create a plan for how to share your response. It is essential that you respond to student feedback when they've taken the time and mustered the courage to share it with you.

1. Start by highlighting the positive feedback they gave you, focusing on trends you noticed or things that surprised you.

2. Thank them for their constructive criticism and explain any immediate or future changes you're planning to make as a result of their feedback.

3. Acknowledge any student suggestions or requests you will not be implementing and explain your reasoning so students know that you carefully considered their feedback and value their opinions, even if there are other factors at work in your decision-making process.

4. Finally, let students know when the next feedback opportunity will be so they understand this is an ongoing process and you are eager to hear their feedback again soon. Convey to your students that you want to partner with them to build the learning experience together.

How's Your Sleep?

One of the quotes Rebekah posted in her classroom was something she first encountered at her yoga studio: "What you pay attention to will thrive." There's a double meaning here: yes, the desirable things you nurture will grow, but also the undesirable things you fixate on will multiply and fester. Consider the following:

◆ Are you fixating on policies, practices, or people that are keeping you up at night?

◆ Is your dissatisfaction with your homework policy or grading system festering?

◆ Are you having nightmares about classroom management challenges?

◆ Where are you working really hard but not necessarily seeing the results you want?

◆ What are you paying attention to, and how is your attention allowing those issues to thrive?

◆ What might happen if you changed nothing but where you directed your attention?

◆ Where else might you direct that attention instead?

◆ What changes might be more sustainable for you and more effective for your students?

These are clues about what may be burning you out and how you may be able to reframe your mental and emotional responses to those things, even if practical changes are not yet possible.

Connecting Instruction and Classroom Management

In the first few years of many educators' careers, the number one thing on their minds is classroom management: How do I ensure students stay focused? How do I make sure my students behave? One thing that all educators need to remember is that classroom management is directly connected to the instructional plan and expectations for learning. It can be a true professional turning point when a teacher fully embraces the idea that strong instruction is the best classroom management. If you are struggling with classroom management, the most important thing you can do is focus on your instruction. Seek out mentors, coaches, and peers who can help you assess why your students are not accessing and engaging with the curriculum as you hope. Any classroom management system you implement without a clear understanding of cause and effect is unlikely to produce long-term results.

At the same time, some teachers find that having a separate rewards-based classroom management system helps their students be successful. Here are a few tips for effective reward systems:

◆ Before you implement a reward system, discuss it with your students and have all systems set up.

◆ The system to track student success should be simple and not take up too much of the teacher's time.

◆ The specific behaviors the teacher is working to reduce must be clear and should be discussed with the students.

◆ If students receive a reward, it should not be taken from them even if they have a negative interaction after they received the reward. The student did something positive to get the reward and that should not be taken away.

◆ Give the system a try for at least two weeks before giving up on it or making big changes. You might have to make small tweaks but sticking with it will show your students they can count on you to be consistent and trust you at your word.

Use the Reflective Tool for Designing Classroom Systems in the appendix and at https://www.wiley.com/go/educating passionpurpose for further planning and analysis of classroom procedures and routines. While this resource might be especially useful for early-career educators who are working to design their classroom environments, we've found that more experienced teachers also benefit from reflecting on their classroom systems each year to identify what's already working well and what might work even better for students. Additionally, teacher teams who use the same classroom systems can work through the tool together.

What If You're Still Learning How to Teach?

First of all, we're *all* still learning how to teach! Education is a research-based field, so we're all in a constant state of growth as we continuously understand more about how students learn best. Indeed, we have all chosen to be in the profession of teaching and learning, and we are the lead learners in our schools, classrooms, and districts. But if you are in the first years of your career in education, this is exactly the right time to focus on your instructional philosophy and practice. Reflecting on your purpose will help to ensure your pedagogical skills are developing in alignment with your *why*, potentially preventing future conflicts that challenge your personal sense of authenticity and integrity and might lead to burnout. See Chapter 5 for much more on embracing a learner mindset.

Additional Considerations for Leaders

Clear Structures and Expectations Help Everyone

One of the most important roles of the school leader is to have a vision and ensure there are systems and structures set up in the school that support the vision. Clear schoolwide policies mean teachers can spend their time focusing on instruction; the more the administrative staff takes responsibility for creating and enforcing schoolwide policies, the more time teachers have to focus on teaching. At the same time, this work must be collaborative so teachers feel empowered to engage with these policies and students receive clear, consistent messaging from all adults. When there are clear policies set up within the school addressing student behaviors, homework, late work policies, grading, and so on, then all educators within the building can be consistent. When creating these systems and structures the leader must create a forum to allow all stakeholders to have a voice in the decision-making process, and it is essential that when hiring new staff members these policies are discussed in the interviewing process to ensure new staff members are clear and on board with the expectations and policies. When teachers do not have to burden themselves creating compliance-based procedures and structures, they can focus on what is most important, which is instruction and curriculum. Here are a few questions to think about when creating these policies:

- ◆ **Student Behavior Expectations:** What are the expectations for student behavior? What is considered "misbehavior"? How should teachers address student misbehaviors? When should a teacher be allowed to ask a student to leave the classroom? Where do students go when they leave the room? What follow-up do teachers need to have once they have asked a student to leave the room? Who do they contact when they need help with student behaviors? Who is responsible for contacting families when a student misbehaves?

- ◆ **Homework Policies:** What is the purpose of homework? Is there a maximum amount of time for how long students should work on homework each night? Are expectations age- and grade-appropriate? What resources do students need access to before you assign homework? How should homework impact a student's grade?

◆ **Late Work Policies:** Should students lose points if their work is late? Can late work be handed in? Is there a time in the semester or marking period where late work should not be submitted? Is there any harm in letting students hand in work late, as it still shows evidence of student learning?

◆ **Grading Policies:** What is the purpose of a grade at your school? Are students graded on effort, mastery, or other performance indicators? How are homework and other student tasks completed outside of class time weighted? Are standardized test scores included in students' grades?

Feedback Is Essential

School leaders should have procedures in place to evaluate systems and structures to ensure students and staff have the opportunity to share open feedback. Teachers need to be empowered to give feedback on whether they are spending too much of their day on things that are not directly connected to student achievement and learning. Here are a few possibilities:

◆ At the end of team meetings, engage teachers in a closing reflection routine. What did they get out of the meeting? What are their takeaways? What are their action steps? These responses should be documented and revisited at the beginning of the next meeting.

◆ We recommend that school leaders establish a cabinet of leaders representing a variety of school teams along with students to have open discussions of policies and procedures that impact the school. This team should meet at least once a month to ensure the leader has a clear understanding of the school community. For this to be successful, the members of the team need to feel safe and need to see that their voices and ideas are heard and taken into consideration when making decisions for the school community.

◆ The school leader also should have a mechanism for anonymous feedback from all stakeholders. This can be as simple as having a suggestion box in their main office with a template people can use to put feedback in or it can be sending out surveys monthly to your community.

Notes

1. Coates, T. (2015). *Between the World and Me*. New York: Spiegel & Grau.
2. Quoted in Howard, J. (1963). Doom and glory of knowing who you are. *Life Magazine* (24 May), p. 89. https://books.google.com/books?id=mEkEAAAAMBAJ&lpg=PA89&vq=unprecedented&pg=PA88#v=onepage&q&f=false (accessed 25 November 2022).

Chapter 5

Being the Lead Learner

"Teachers who are learners create a safe space for students to express themselves and do not shut down students who have a different perspective or a different way of tackling things. Instead, they ask questions to understand the different method/perspective."
—Martha, Class of 2010

We believe a teacher's most important job is to be the lead learner in their classroom. Often, when educators talk about learning, they're talking about professional development (PD). But because we know PD looks different in different places, and some teachers don't even have formal opportunities for PD, we're focusing here on learning more broadly. In this chapter, we explain how we have fueled our purposes through learning from many different sources, including mentors, travel, summer employment, and yes, even PD.

What's the connection between leaning into learning and addressing burnout? One antidote to the sense of stagnation that often accompanies burnout is the fire of curiosity. By continuing to ask questions and seek answers about your *why*, you'll build, develop, and strengthen your sense of purpose. Embracing the identity of lead learner can show you the kind of educator you're passionate about being. Stay curious about your purpose so you can learn more about how to live and work in alignment with it.

We also want to take a moment to address the question of learning during summer vacation, especially within the context of burnout. Just like yoga, meditation, or whatever you enjoy doing for a little R&R, your summer vacation isn't going to fix everything even if it provides a temporary break from the conditions that are burning you out. While we wholeheartedly encourage educators to see summer as a respite from what can be an incredibly exhausting and stressful job, we believe summer is also an opportunity to embrace a lead learner mindset and to engage in self-directed learning that deepens your connection to your purpose by exploring your own passions. However, summer is one time for learning, but it's not the only time. Regardless of what time of year it is, thinking of yourself as a learner first will keep you connected to the teaching and learning experience you are designing and facilitating every day.

Case in point: In the summer of 2006, the two of us traveled together to California and then Hawaii. For the first week, we attended a full-time teaching institute in the Los Angeles area. It was a lot like traditional PD, with expert educators leading us through readings, classroom simulations, collaborative planning, peer feedback, and exam scoring practice. We sat at desks, took notes, and diligently reflected on how we would apply what we learned. The next week we flew to Maui. (Because we both lived in New York City, LA was halfway to Hawaii, and we couldn't resist the opportunity for a trip to paradise.) It was a vacation in every sense of that word, but not from learning. Because we never really turn off our teacher brains, we were constantly learning during that week, whether by trekking through the rainforest, being the oldest students at surf school, or traveling to the top of a volcano to watch the sunrise and then biking all the way down. That trip was both restful and enriching. We believe summer can and should be both for all educators, and you don't have to travel to Hawaii to make that happen.

What we reflect on in this chapter:

- What Meredith learned from challenging situations as both a student and a school leader.

- How Rebekah used her summers for personal professional learning, including when she taught summer school.

- How we collaborated as teachers to lead a year of faculty PD at our school.

What we hope you take away from this chapter:

- What it means to be a lead learner, especially when it comes to your sense of purpose.

- How to think expansively about PD and professional learning so you can continue to grow no matter what.

- A sense of empowerment about affecting change within your locus of control as a learner.

Meredith's Turn

Pushing Myself as a Learner

I have always needed to push myself to be a learner and learning did not come easy to me. As a student it was so hard for me to learn to read and write at my grade level. I was always behind and needed to figure out ways to improve my skills even after I graduated high school.

When I entered college, I knew I was not the best writer and I knew when I read texts I did not get the deep meaning of these texts compared to other students in my classes. I knew the only way I would be a successful teacher is if I took control of these learning issues and developed my confidence within the class-room. During my freshman year at the University of Vermont, I advocated for myself to be in a special writing class that had an extra lab component attached to the class. When I spoke to my advisor, I remember telling her I needed this class and even if the lab was not credited I needed extra help and I would take it seriously. This extra support was extremely helpful and I learned all about the power of the writing center.

As a freshman in college, I took a literature seminar that focused on African American literature with Professor Diouf. This course was a small class with fewer than 20 students and it was designed as a seminar, so students would read at home and come to class and discuss the themes of the different texts. We were reading Toni Morrison's *Beloved* and I tried to read this text for its understanding but I was struggling constantly. There were so many times in class when I did not fully understand the reading from the week before and I would listen to the deep analysis of my classmates and I was so envious of their knowledge and ability to articulate it. I always tried to stay quiet in class and just took notes. I remember going back to my dorm after class and rereading the section we had covered over and over again. I never got the same meaning as my classmates.

Then there was one day I came into class and Professor Diouf announced that instead of discussing the meaning we would write about it. He explained we could use the text if we needed it but we could not use our notes. I took out my copy of *Beloved* and my loose-leaf paper and I felt like I was looking at another language that I could not understand. At that moment, I just looked down at my paper and began to cry. Professor Diouf asked me to step outside to speak to me and it was that moment where I explained to him that I was trying to understand the reading and I showed him my annotated text, but the truth was I did not fully understand the meaning and connections the other students so clearly articulated in all of our discussions. I told him I could not handle the pressure of the timed writing and I just did not know what to do. He looked at me and told me not to worry and that meaning will come with time. He told me it was up to me to find the meaning and that I could write whatever I was thinking. His belief in me and allowing me to make my own interpretations without the pressures of a correct answer gave me the spirit to at least go back in and try. I do not remember what I got on that paper but I do remember gaining just a little bit of confidence in my thoughts and it taught me that it would be my job to inspire and believe in each and every one of my students as Professor Diouf did for me.

During my senior year at UVM, I took another class with Professor Diouf but this time it was a larger lecture-style class with 40 to 50 students. For this course on African History, the end assignment for the course was to give a presentation about a contemporary issue in a specific part of Africa and an analysis of possible resolutions. For this I wrote about the Global GAG rule and its impact on Kenyan Women. After I presented, I wanted to go up to Professor Diouf and tell him I was that student who cried in his class four years earlier, but I figured there was no way he would remember me. And then when class was coming to an end, he stood up and called three names out, mine included, and he said we all needed to stay after class. When it was my turn to speak to him, he said mine was the best presentation he had ever heard in his class and he was so eager to read my paper. He also told me that yes, he did remember me and he wanted me to be proud of how far I had come. I was so honored and happy he took the time to talk to me and acknowledge my growth. This is something I strive to do with my students and staff through my journey of education. I try to support those I work with and speak out when I know they are trying so hard to reach their goals. I felt empowered walking out of this class as a senior and just one step closer to tackling my own learning struggles by continually pushing myself to learn and grow.

Another essential part of my growth as a learner was my decision to join the debate team at UVM. As a high school student, I would get extremely nervous when I was called on to share in class and I completely feared reading aloud in class. I will never forget the feeling that came over my entire body when the teacher would tell the class to open to a specific page and say that we will "popcorn" read. This is when one student starts reading and then stops whenever they wanted to and calls on the next student. My heart would pound and I would completely shut down. I always tried to read ahead of the student just in case they called on me. I became fixated, nervous, and had complete tunnel vision on how I would accomplish this task and I was not able to comprehend anything. If I was called on, I would begin to get panic attacks inside and for some classes my friends knew I would not read a lot when a teacher called on me, so they would just begin reading if my name was called.

When I got to college and was in my education classes, I knew I needed to do something to force myself to grow as I knew I would reach my goal of being a teacher and I would have to read aloud to my students. This is when I made the decision to join the UVM debate team. This was one of the biggest decisions I ever made in my true development as a learner. The debate team gave me the opportunity to read publicly, speak in front of people, develop deep comprehension skills, and grow my confidence with an amazing team of peers and coaches. The beauty of debate is that when I was reading, we would speed read, so if I made a mistake in my reading, I was the only one who knew it. As well, it allowed me to speak my mind and see that when you are passionate about a topic, you can use your voice to speak up in front of people. I was able to use these skills when I got in front of my classroom.

It is through all these experiences that I learned the importance of always being open to learning and growing. As educators, we need to continue to push ourselves for the betterment of our students. I also always want my students to know the power of learning and to never give up on their goals. We need to create schools that empower our young learners to be themselves and support their needs.

Professional Development within the School Setting

In the 2012–2013 school year, Rebekah and I had the opportunity to be the lead teachers within the school community. With this we got an increased responsibility: to run professional development. This impacted and transformed my thinking of how a school community can use PD time to grow and learn as a community.

At this point in our careers, we both had been through a lot of PD and we were very aware of what our school community needed. We spent a lot of time planning for these sessions with the goal that our teachers would feel like this time was well spent, they would walk out with a specific strategy they could implement within their classroom, and they would have structured time to work with their colleagues to discuss the school-wide instructional focus and apply it directly to what they were teaching. There are a few things we did to ensure this was a productive time for all educators within our building. We sent emails to our staff prior to PD to let them know what our focus was and reminded them to bring planning materials they could apply to the topic. During the sessions, we practiced a specific teaching strategy with the staff they could apply directly to their lessons the next day or as soon as they felt it matched the learning goal. We also had our staff give us feedback after every session. Before we planned the next session, we reviewed that feedback and work to incorporate it into our next session.

The most powerful part of our professional development each semester was when we brought students into the session to model a teaching strategy and then our teachers were able to ask the students for specific feedback on the strategy and they would get ideas on how they could modify the strategy for their classroom. We also planned backward based on where we wanted teachers to be by the end of the semester and year. As one of the leaders of this work, I found it essential that I had a thought partner who helped push my thinking and this made me a better teacher in my classroom. Rebekah and I had very different styles of teaching in our classrooms but when it came to leading our staff, we were able to collaboratively create an authentic learning community. This experience pushed me in my last two years of teaching and inspired me to be the leader I am today.

My First Lesson as a Principal

I will never forget one of my first staff meetings as the new principal of my school. I had been working in the school for the past 13 years as a teacher and assistant principal, but this was my first year as the principal and it was one of the first full staff meetings for the year. As a staff, we were norming our expectations for our students and the topic of headwear came up. I do believe it is important to be able to see our students' eyes and ears in class to ensure they are alert and focused. This is why we always had a policy that students cannot wear hoodies in classes, but we enforced this inconsistently. This year I decided for the first time that we would allow students to wear hats, but we would not have students wear hoodies or head wraps, specifically durags, in class. I went into this meeting not thinking it would be controversial. I was not thinking about the cultural implication of a white principal standing in front of my diverse staff saying, we will allow students to wear hats, but we will inform students they have to remove their hoodies and head wraps.

This led to my staff asking very deep questions and expressing that this policy is not culturally responsive and equitable to our male students. If we allow our female students to wear head wraps, then we should allow our male students to wear durags. I had a few staff members get extremely emotional as they told stories about how important their head wraps are to them and it is not just a religious reason. It is for style, culture, and their own identity. During the meeting, I stopped talking and started listening. I ended the meeting and informed my staff I would take all of this information and email everyone with a policy we would follow starting the next day, as it was the first day of school for students. During this moment, I got very emotional as my intention was not to strip my students or staff from their identity, but without thinking about the impact of the policy, I was in fact doing this. In a situation like this it does not matter my intention, rather it matters the impact. This was an example of a time when I was naive on the cultural implications of a policy and I needed time to reflect, respond, and lead. Here is the email I sent to my staff the evening following this meeting:

> Good evening-
> First, I want to say thank you for all of your honesty and passion in the meeting this afternoon. I know that this year will be a transformative year, especially if we stick together.
> I have been thinking about the policies that are most important for our students to be successful and for us to reach our school goals. It is clear that the policy for headgear is controversial. Our community vision is a place where our students are present and engaged in class. I believe that hats, hoodies, and headphones distract our students and impair their ability to be fully present in class. I also feel that after further reflection and review of the Chancellor's Regulations, durags and scarfs are not

*inherently disruptive to the educational process and to be true to the
mission for this year, this policy must change.*

*To be clear, the following items cannot be worn in class: headphones,
hats, hoodies (up and over heads). In talking to students, you should
emphasize that we must be able to see and hear one another to be active
and productive in class discussions and assignments.*

*Our community functions best when we keep our collective calling
in mind: to provide an encouraging and supportive environment in
which our students can grow and learn. It was made clear this afternoon
that we all hold this mission close to heart, and I believe this policy will
reflect our beliefs in our students. As always, my door is open and I look
forward to your continued passion for improving our community.*

It is the relationships that I have built with my students and
colleagues throughout these years that drive me to be a better
person and leader. I want to continue to work to break down
barriers that exist within our society that have led to a clear
difference of opportunity for myself and my students. I need to
name the difference, recognize it, and continue to open up the
conversation among white and BIPOC students and staff. It is
essential to recognize that, as educators, we cannot opt out of the
conversation. We need to sit in our discomfort and use it as a
time to reflect. We must continue to educate, speak up, and
advocate to break down the systems that perpetuate the white
supremacist structures that our education system was founded
on to ensure every student is educated in an equitable system.

Rebekah's Turn

Professional Learning That's Personal and Purposeful

My sense of purpose is grounded in my belief that all learners
should have access to joyful, vibrant, enchanting, empowering
learning experiences. As I've shared, that belief grew out of my
experience as a student with a disconnect between schooling and
learning, and my conviction that all young people should
experience school as a place where they get to learn the things
they want to learn in the ways they want to learn them, not only
where adults tell them what and how to learn.

Perhaps unsurprisingly, therefore, throughout my career as an
educator I have always thought of myself as a learner first and
have been drawn to opportunities to explore and experiment.
These ongoing learning experiences have made me a better
teacher by keeping me immersed in the learning process.

Because I'm always searching for new ways to learn, I never feel "done." Learning on my own has always been a year-round pursuit, whether that meant embracing my own joyful, vibrant, enchanting, empowering learning experiences during the school day, after school, or over the summer.

Starting in my first years as a teacher, I applied for grants and fellowships and brought that learning back to my students. Whether I was studying with Shakespeare scholars in Stratford-upon-Avon, retracing my grandparents' 1983 journey through Soviet-era Hungary, training preservice teachers in the Bronx, or working in a vegan restaurant for my culinary school internship, I saw the world as my classroom, and I wanted my students to feel the same way.

These experiences, especially but not exclusively during my summer vacations, have kept me excited about teaching, immersed in the process of learning, and inspired to keep enhancing the learning experiences I design and facilitate for others since I was an early-career teacher. I was still in graduate school during the summer after my first year as a teacher, so I had to wait until the following year to really feel like I had a true summer vacation. Inspired by a teacher friend's experience in the same program, I participated in what was then called a National Endowment for the Humanities Summer Seminar for Teachers. As a member of this 15-person team of educators from all over the country, I spent three weeks at the University of Delaware learning from Shakespeare scholars and then traveled to Stratford-upon-Avon, Shakespeare's birthplace, for two additional weeks. In Stratford we toured historical sites and saw a show by the Royal Shakespeare Company every night. It was my first experience with professional development as immersive, choice-based, and site-specific.

I was hooked on using my summers to learn from people and places that inspired me, so when my mom discovered a type-written travel journal my grandmother had kept when she and my grandfather road-tripped through Hungary, Austria, and Italy in 1983 to trace their own roots and connect with distant relatives, I recreated their itinerary and mapped their journey as closely as I could. Two summers later, my mom and I set out to retrace my grandparents' steps, meeting in Budapest for a road trip throughout Hungary to visit all the places my grandparents had gone, even staying in the same hotels when we could. When we returned to Budapest, my mom flew back to Miami, and I continued on my own via the Danube River, as my grandparents had done 25 years earlier, past Bratislava (probably sailing right under the bridge that Meredith introduced to her students on the first day of school) to Vienna, and then over the next couple of weeks by train through Austria and Italy until I got to Rome.

Even though I no longer have summer vacations, I still travel to learn as frequently as I can, turning vacations into historical-cultural learning tours. One year, I took a road trip through Georgia and Alabama to visit sites associated with the Civil Rights Movement. These were places where Black Americans and activists of other races fought back against oppression. Immersing myself in that history and the embodied fortitude of the people who were actually there was powerful. Visiting historical sites—not just in the American South but elsewhere, too—has impacted my understanding of history and culture in ways I never would have from books and school alone.

Summer Schooling

I've done plenty of classroom learning on my own time, but I think I've learned more about teaching and learning from being a student in subjects that had nothing to do with conventional education than I ever did from more typical professional learning experiences. Since childhood, I've been an avid cook and baker, and one of the most profound learning moments of my professional life came during a cake decorating class I took one summer. I was having some trouble making icing flowers, and I asked the pastry chef for help. "Can you show me the first part again?" I asked. "Well, it's not a difficult part," she quipped while demonstrating the way to curl the icing as she twirled the rose in her other hand. It was an instant gut punch. *Ouch*, I thought. It was difficult for *me*. But in the next moment I felt an even more painful jab: I had likely made my own students feel that way many, many times. Countlessly I had said things to my classes like "Okay people, it's not a rocket ship" or "Let's pick up the pace everyone" or "You should know this by now." How many of my students had thought to themselves, "*Ouch*. It might as well be a rocket ship to *me*?" I had enrolled in that class to learn cake decorating techniques, but I left with a greater understanding of what it was like to be a struggling student, a far more enduring takeaway than any marzipan banana I molded that week.

For me, the best way to use my summer vacations was to reconnect to my identity as a learner, so I generally did not take summer jobs or teach summer school when I was a classroom teacher. I realize this is a privilege that many educators don't have and the opportunity to earn additional money over the summer is not something all of us can afford to pass up. On occasion I did work over the summer, but I made sure I would be learning as well as earning during those experiences and that they would still provide me with the mental break I always desperately needed by the end of the school year. When I did teach summer school, I insisted I be able to design the course around New York City-based texts with an immersive, half-day schedule so I could take my students on field trips every day. As a result, I got to experiment with teaching texts and topics through experiences I couldn't easily facilitate during the school year. Instead of feeling even more drained and exhausted as the new school year approached, I was excited to incorporate experiential learning into my classroom and rejuvenated by the opportunities I had earlier in the summer to experiment, fail, and try again with an outside-the-box curriculum.

However, teaching summer school was never something that filled me up the way that most of my other summer activities did. Instead, when I needed to earn additional income during the summer, I tried to do it in other ways. One summer I worked for the New York City Teaching Fellows, the alternative certification program I had participated in as a beginning teacher. Each morning I traveled throughout the Bronx visiting the 20 or so preservice teachers I was supervising, and in the afternoons I taught workshops on the real-life skills they would need when they led their own classrooms that September: lesson planning, classroom management, organization, instructional skills, even how to understand their paycheck deductions. It was physically and intellectually arduous, and there was emotional labor, too, in supporting them through the realization that they had just signed up for the hardest job they would ever have, but I loved it. Teaching others how to teach helped me clarify and codify my own beliefs and understandings about teaching, and visiting other schools and classrooms and collaborating with the other advisors were enriching learning experiences that helped me to grow because I was outside of my usual professional environment.

Your Turn

Who Are You as a Learner?

As educators, we often talk about the importance of understanding how our individual students learn best, but we also need to understand how we learn best, too. When we're aware of our own learning needs, we're more equipped to engage in our professional learning community and to modify our environment to best support those needs.

1. How do you learn best? Do you need to read, write, talk, listen, move, experience, draw, or create to understand something new?

2. To what extent have your professional learning experiences aligned with how you learn best? How have those experiences impacted you and your students as a result?

3. What have been your most effective learning experiences? What made them so effective?

4. What have been your least effective learning experiences? What would have made them more effective?

What Do You Need to Learn to Fuel Your Purpose? How Do You Need to Learn It?

Think back to the purpose you articulated in Chapter 1. By continuing to ask questions and seek answers about your *why*, you'll build, develop, and strengthen your sense of purpose and your ability to live and work in alignment with it.

1. If time and money were not factors, what would you like to learn? How would you like to learn it?

2. What fills your tank as an educator? Where do your motivation, inspiration, and resilience come from? What do you do when you need to recharge?

3. What would you like to learn to deepen your sense of purpose? What experiences might help you better understand how to live and work in alignment with it?

4. What does it look like to be the lead learner in your classroom? What do your students need you to learn?

For a version of this activity that's especially useful as summer vacation approaches, see the Intentional Summer Planning Protocol in the appendix and at https://www.wiley.com/go/educatingpassionpurpose. You might try completing it several times throughout the spring semester to see how your summer vision evolves over time.

What Do You Have Control of When It Comes to Your Learning?

We know PD looks different in different places, and some teachers don't even have formal opportunities for PD, which is why we've focused on learning more broadly. Think about all the opportunities you have to learn, both in school and out of school, during the school year, and over the summer, and so on.

1. To what extent do you have a voice in what PD looks like at your school? Are there opportunities for you to share feedback, take a leadership role, or otherwise help shape what your in-school professional learning experience is?

2. How do you want to contribute to the profession both in and beyond your school? Are there opportunities for you to participate in coaching, mentoring, inter-visitations, conferences, virtual events, social media communities, and other ecosystems that support teacher-driven professional learning?

3. How might you use time beyond the regular school day and year for learning that enriches and inspires you? For example, what would it look like to fuel your purpose during the summer, even if you are working?

What If the PD at Your School Isn't Adequate?

We firmly believe a lead learner can learn anywhere, even if it's about learning what not to do. But that is cold comfort when you're staring down 10 months of weekly sessions that feel irrelevant or pointless. Start by considering why PD is not effective for you (and others, if this is a shared opinion). Is it the content? The format? The facilitation? The timing? The location? The grouping? Once you have a sense of what specifically makes PD ineffective, you can start to think about what you have control over and what you can do about it.

In our experience working with schools, the most destructive belief that negatively impacts a professional learning community is the misunderstanding that PD has to involve the entire faculty learning together at the same time in the same way, such as a standard weekly session for all teachers. In many cases, teachers feel like PD is pointless because they aren't given opportunities for choice, agency, differentiation, and flexibility. We know these are the characteristics of strong classroom instruction for students, and they are features of effective professional learning, too. If you suspect that PD is ineffective at your school because the people in charge subscribe to this limiting belief, think about what power you have to challenge that belief, advocate for change, and play a role in transforming what professional learning looks like at your school.

We strongly encourage teachers to take ownership of their learning whenever they can. This looks different in every school, and might include volunteering for a leadership position in your school's professional learning community, joining the team that designs and facilitates learning, identifying a buddy to push your thinking in new ways, meeting with your school leaders to offer feedback and suggest changes, sharing how you learn on your own, or other empowering acts of self-advocacy.

The Teacher-Led Inquiry Cycle for Professional Development resource in the appendix and at https://www.wiley.com/go/educatingpassionpurpose provides an example of what teacher-centered PD can look like, but there are lots of other iterations you may adapt or consider. An Internet search for "teacher inquiry cycle" will give you a range of options.

What If You Just Need a Break?

Take a break! You're human and if you're feeling anxious, depressed, or overwhelmed, then you might not be at your best for your students. A break of some kind can be just the thing that reenergizes you for your students and your community. That might mean taking a mental health day, saying no to additional responsibilities, setting all work aside over the weekend or during a school vacation, putting an auto-reply on your email and not checking in outside of certain times, or taking the summer off. But if you find these breaks aren't enough to recharge you, then you may need to consider making more significant changes that are sustainable and enduring. And that's, of course, what this whole book is about! One way to think about this with respect to taking a break is to reflect on exactly what kind of break you need. As described in this chapter, we've found lots of ways to take a break from the daily grind of the school year while still strengthening our teaching practice through learning experiences that are meaningful for us. The same may be true for you.

What If You Need Time to Reconnect with Family and Friends?

Reconnect! Teaching is way more than a full-time job. If you're feeling lonely or isolated, reconnecting with your loved ones can help you feel supported and cared for when you need it most. (But be sure to avoid those people you have toxic or unhealthy relationships with—some of whom you might be related to. You might find you need to disconnect from those people to safeguard your mental health.) Rebekah's friend Carolyn is a district administrator who travels between her office and her network's schools on a daily basis. She uses these commutes to catch up with friends and family around the country. These 15-minute conversations provide the perfect opportunity to check in and stay in touch. See Chapter 7 for more on building your personal support system.

What If You Need a Change of Scenery?

That depends on what you mean by "scenery." We're probably not alone in our love of vacations, especially tropical ones, but travel isn't always possible for many reasons. We're also big fans of staycations and of exploring new and unfamiliar locations in our own communities, like Rebekah does with her weekly field trips:

When the pandemic started and my husband and I both began working from home, our 600-square-foot apartment became unbearably stifling. The summer of 2020 provided a respite because we could be outside, and because museums reopened at reduced capacity, but as the fall approached, I knew I needed a plan for how I was going to protect both my productivity and my mental health as the weather changed. I decided I would take a field trip every Wednesday afternoon. I would block off my calendar for art. When my field trip project began in the fall of 2020, it was still warm enough for me to be outside, so I started with something I had wanted to do for a while and that to this day, more than two years into my weekly field trip routine, is still my absolute favorite: a sound walk of Brooklyn's Green-Wood Cemetery created by Gelsey Bell.[1] I was enthralled by what I experienced that afternoon, and I spent the subway ride home thinking about what it would be like for students to create sound walks in their own neighborhoods even amidst the pandemic. I was so excited about this

*idea that I emailed Gelsey, and I gushed about the whole experience to a Boston
school leader I was coaching remotely, who then developed the sound walk into a
project that some of his students completed in their own neighborhoods. Investing in my own learning across the city where I live has taught me so much about
how to be a better teacher and leader.*

On the other hand, if the "scenery" you need to change is
your whole school, we have an entire chapter on that coming
up next!

What If You Need to Earn Extra Money?

While we advocate that educators use their time away from
school to deepen their own learning and sense of purpose, we
know this may be a luxury for teachers who need to prioritize
their financial well-being. As described in this chapter, we've
both taken on lots of additional jobs, both after school and over
the summer, to earn extra money. By coaching preservice teachers, adjunct teaching at local graduate schools of education, and
grading exams, in addition to teaching outside-the-box summer
school courses, we've been able to boost our bank accounts while
also beating burnout. Our hope is that you'll be able to find ways
to turn that extra work into learning, too.

What If You Need to Provide Childcare?

If you have children of your own who have the same vacations
you do, then it may feel like you have no personal time to
invest in your own learning, but generating interesting summer experiences for your kids could be an entry point for
opportunities to enhance your own learning, too. Is there a field
trip, science experiment, art activity, new book, or creative
topic you've always wanted to share with your students but
have never had the time to put together? Pilot the experience
with your family to check things out and get a sense of
how your students might respond so you can plan for the
future. Even if your students and your own children are not
the same age, testing things out with a small audience can
be helpful in allowing you to predict what works and how
to make the experience as effective as possible for
your students.

What If You've Been Assigned a Mentor You're Not Learning From?

Our hope for all educators is that they'll have opportunities for job-embedded professional learning, including working with a highly effective mentor who challenges, supports, and gets them. But we also know this is not always the case and many teachers are paired with peers or mentors who are not an ideal fit for lots of reasons. In our experience, the number one reason assigned mentoring relationships aren't helpful is that mentors rarely receive training in how to effectively coach and provide feedback to their peers. Instead, the assumption is that because they are a strong or experienced teacher, they will be able to impart their knowledge and skills to their colleagues automatically. But this is actually an entirely different skill set, and many mentors don't know how to share their expertise with others effectively. As a result, mentoring meetings can turn into venting sessions, lectures, or laundry lists of suggested improvements, not because the mentor doesn't want to be helpful but because they're not sure how to be better.

If you're receiving ineffective mentoring, think about the reflective questions you answered earlier in this chapter about how you learn best and identify which elements of your learning style it would be helpful to share with your mentor. For example, if you really need to see an example of something before you're able to do it, ask if you can visit their class to watch them teach. If you learn best by doing, invite them to visit your class. You can also seek out mentors on your own. Meredith has had powerful learning experiences with colleagues who were both assigned to her and who she cultivated an informal mentorship with.

If you're a mentor who fears you're not providing your colleague with the support they need, our most important suggestion is to invest in your own professional learning to strengthen your skills. If training is available in your district or community, seek it out. If there are other mentors in your school or district who seem to have a stronger impact, build relationships so you can learn from and with them. We especially recommend the coaching resources developed and facilitated by Elena Aguilar and the Bright Morning Team, including her book *The Art of Coaching*.

See Chapter 7 as well as the Mentor Matching and Reflection Tool in the appendix and at https://www.wiley.com/go/educat ingpassionpurpose for a resource to help establish effective mentoring relationships. This tool can be used by administrators who are tasked with assigning mentoring pairs and by the teachers in those mentoring pairs as they begin their work together.

What If PD Is Causing Your Burnout?

You probably know what we're going to say here. The antidote to burnout is purpose. This isn't just because it can remind you about what's really important to you and possibly allow you to put your disappointing or frustrating PD experiences into perspective. It's because standing in your purpose can provide you with a litmus test for decision-making. If the support, development, and learning opportunities you're offered at your school aren't aligned with your purpose, it might be time for a change of some kind. When the two of us took over PD at our school, created a year-long curriculum, and started facilitating weekly sessions, it wasn't because our principal asked us to. It was because we volunteered. We were not satisfied with the PD offerings at our school, and we wanted to do something about it. Because of the nature of our positions, we had additional time in our schedule for this, and we're not sharing this example because we think all teachers who are dissatisfied with PD can or should volunteer to run it themselves. But in our case, doing so was very much aligned with our purposes around prioritizing relationships and ensuring vibrant learning experiences for all learners, including our adult colleagues.

If being forced to engage in PD that's misaligned with your purpose is contributing to your sense of burnout, you have a duty to yourself to try to do something about that. The most extreme action you may be able to take is to move to a different work environment where the professional learning culture is more consistent with your sense of purpose. That may feel like a daunting change to make, which is why we have a whole chapter on it coming up next!

Reading to Learn

The following recommended reading list highlights some of the most powerful books and experts we have learned from in our ongoing journeys toward becoming anti-racist educators. It would be impossible for us to list everything we've read and certainly everything you may read, so we encourage you to explore, research, and find the teachers who are right for you as you move forward on your own unique journey. Note that some of these writers work with organizations that offer in-person and virtual trainings, and we highly recommend opportunities to learn directly from them and their teams when possible.

Alphabetical by title:

- *All the Real Indians Died Off: And 20 Other Myths about Native Americans*, Roxanne Dunbar-Ortiz and Dina Gilio-Whitaker.
- *Between the World and Me*, Ta-Nehisi Coates.
- *Coaching for Equity*, Elena Aguilar.
- *Courageous Conversations About Race: A Field Guide for Achieving Equity in Schools and Beyond*, Glenn E. Singleton.
- *Cultivating Genius: An Equity Framework for Culturally and Historically Responsive Literacy*, Gholdy Muhammad.
- *Culturally Responsive Teaching and the Brain: Promoting Authentic Engagement and Rigor Among Culturally and Linguistically Diverse Students*, Zaretta L. Hammond.
- *Emergent Strategy*, adrienne maree brown.
- *Grading for Equity: What It Is, Why It Matters, and How It Can Transform Schools and Classrooms*, Joe Feldman.
- *How to Be an Antiracist*, Ibram X. Kendi.
- *An Indigenous Peoples' History of the United States for Young People*, Roxanne Dunbar-Ortiz, Jean Mendoza, and Debbie Reese.
- *Me and White Supremacy*, Layla Saad.
- *Pushout: The Criminalization of Black Girls in Schools*, Monique Morris.
- *Stamped: Racism, Antiracism, and You: A Remix of the National Book Award-Winning Stamped from the Beginning*, Jason Reynolds and Ibram X. Kendi.
- *This Book Is Anti-Racist: 20 Lessons on How to Wake Up, Take Action, and Do the Work*, Tiffany Jewell and Aurelia Durand.
- *White Fragility: Why It's So Hard for White People to Talk about Racism*, Robin Diangelo.
- White Supremacy Culture, Tema Okun [https://www .whitesupremacyculture.info/].

Additional Considerations for Leaders

We hope reading through the "Your Turn" section has allowed you to reflect on the learning experiences you offer teachers in your school or district and acquire some possible ideas for adjustments you may make. If not, starting with an anonymous survey to garner feedback from teachers about their professional learning experiences is a great place to begin. As a principal once said to Rebekah, "You can't have student-centered instruction if you don't have teacher-centered PD." If we want classroom learning to be responsive to students' needs, interests, and voices, then we need to do the same for professional learning. Incorporating teachers' voices in PD starts with listening to those voices and really hearing what they have to say.

Here are some additional reflective questions to help school and district leaders think about how they can support teachers as learners:

◆ What does PD look like in your school or district? Do teachers have a voice, leadership, choice, and agency? Do they see the impact of their professional learning in their classrooms?

◆ What do teachers do when they gather together? Is the purpose of those gatherings primarily to learn together? What structures have been established to support collaboration?

◆ In his book *Teach Like a Champion*, Doug Lemov highlights "the joy factor" as a key element of successful classrooms (p. 442).[2] What's true for students is also true for educators. Where is the joy in the PD your teachers experience? How do you make learning engaging, exciting, and joyful for them?

◆ We strongly believe in job-embedded professional learning that leverages the expertise within a school community. Consider the alignment between your PD goals and current practice in your school. Do you have educators who are able to design and lead a professional learning culture that will help all teachers meet those goals? What support and training do those leaders need? When might it be helpful to bring in outside experts to support professional learning?

◆ If your teachers are the lead learners of their classrooms, then you are the lead learner of your school or district. What learning are you engaged in? How do you model a lead learner mindset for the educators you work with? Do you make your growth transparent about how you receive mentoring, read professional texts, attend trainings or conferences, or receive feedback from your own supervisors?

◆ The ultimate way for leaders to model a lead learner mindset is to teach a class of their own. We've both worked with a number of school leaders who have taught students in their school in addition to their administrative responsibilities. Granted, sometimes it's been a bit of a disaster, especially when the administrator is new to their role and the decision to teach a class is based on a scheduling necessity rather than an authentic desire to work directly with students. But when it works, it can be a powerful way to contribute to the professional learning culture. In all the cases we've observed, the administrator is not the strongest teacher in the school—sometimes far from it—but there is no clearer way to tell teachers that you understand them and that you are learning, too. Meredith actually did this. Here's what her experience was like:

I got to co-teach an English class with a new teacher to our community. My role in going back into the classroom was to help the teacher grow and connect to our community, but in the end this opportunity had a large impact on me. It gave me a chance to get back into the classroom, connect with students on a different level than as an administrator, and find passion in literature I had never read before. Co-teaching with Deborah was some of the greatest coaching opportunities of my career. Now in my twenty-first year in education, Deborah is my administrative intern and she continues to push my thinking and we work side by side once again to develop a school community that we strongly believe in for our students. Sometimes the opportunities you least expect are the ones that drive your passion the most.

The Purposeful Planning Tool for Professional Learning in the appendix and at https://www.wiley.com/go/educatingpassion purpose can help you design PD that meets teachers' needs, and we highly recommend using the Professional Learning

Reflection Tool to elicit feedback. Anyone who facilitates professional learning at any level, including the leaders of teacher teams and professional learning communities, can use these resources to design effective adult learning experiences.

Notes

1. Bell, G. (n.d.). *Cairns.* https://www.green-wood.com/cairns/ (accessed 25 November 2022).
2. Lemov, D. (2015). *Teach Like a Champion 2.0.* San Francisco: Jossey-Bass.

Chapter 6

Finding Your Professional Home

> "You can tell when a teacher HATES their job, they have an attitude or may pick on the most redundant things. That has a greater impact on a student's classroom experience because we don't want to be there and if the adult doesn't want to be either, it creates a negative cycle."
> —Cherelinis, Class of 2012

It might seem counterintuitive to focus on hiring and recruitment as a strategy for dealing with burnout. After all, an educator who's struggling with burnout is probably not the best ambassador for their school during the hiring process, and their burnout might be evident to prospective employers if they're looking for a new job themselves. But we've found that getting involved in hiring and recruitment and being proactive about one's own job prospects can go a long way toward avoiding burnout in the first place by kindling the fire of investment in the profession, the long-term health of the school community, and one's own career trajectory.

In thinking about where we work and who we work with, especially through the lens of teacher burnout, we have to consider the intersection of our individual purpose with that of the school's. We believe burnout is primarily caused by misalignment of purpose, whether that be misalignment between our purpose and our actions, or misalignment between our purpose and our school's. The hiring and recruitment process is a key opportunity for examining both individual and institutional purpose, assessing the alignment between them, and taking action to strengthen that alignment.

So how can involvement in the hiring and recruitment process prevent and address burnout? Consider these points:

◆ The hiring process is one component in a long-term strategy to cultivate a transformational learning community. For many educators, being involved in shaping the vision of what their school is and can be is incredibly inspiring and can reinvigorate their passion about and commitment to the school community.

◆ We believe the most important work that happens in a school is the work teachers and students do together in classrooms. Being involved in the teacher hiring process means having a voice in determining who makes up the team that does the most important work at a school and cultivating a culture that promotes transformative student learning. That's exciting!

◆ Playing a role in the hiring and recruitment process actively allows teachers to shape their own teacher teams. What backgrounds, experiences, voices, and energies will create the most effective teams at your school? These folx will be your colleagues, so who do you want to work with?

◆ Thus far we've focused on how to keep the fire going through involvement at your current school, but it's also possible your fire can glow even brighter if you move to a new role or community. You owe it to yourself and all students to be in a position that helps you keep that fire going. If you are burning out, it's time for a change, and that could mean changing positions or schools. We want to acknowledge this might get a little uncomfortable; the prospect of leaving one's school may feel impossible for all sorts of reasons, but we don't think it's helpful to avoid the possibility that sometimes the solution to burnout is a new position that you're even more passionate about.

In this chapter, we share our own stories about being on both sides of the hiring and recruitment process: being hired and doing the hiring.

What we reflect on in this chapter:

◆ The wide range of job-hunting experiences we've had as teachers.

- What we've learned from being on the hiring side of the job-search process.
- What it looks like when the hiring process is aligned with purpose.

What we hope you take away from this chapter:

- How to find the right professional home for you.
- What to do if you realize you're in the wrong place.
- Especially for leaders: how to get the right people in the right place to do the right work.

Meredith's Turn

Each time I left my school and joined a new community it was a big decision for me because I was leaving students and staff I had formed deep relationships with and I wondered if I would ever see them again or learn about their progress in the same way.

The Interview Process Can Tell You about Your New Community

My first interview was a phone interview that lasted 15 to 20 minutes at the most. I was in the Teach for America (TFA) summer institute in Houston, Texas, and I was interviewing for positions in North Carolina. I did not have any control over the interviews I went on. For my first interview, I got on the phone with the principal and she informed me that this year would be her first year at the school and she asked me what I thought about teaching seventh grade English Language Arts and Social Studies. The response I had in my head was I feel great about it—that is why I am here for the call. I of course elaborated on why I was so excited about the opportunity and how I was eager to learn from her community. And then with that she said, great, we start the second to last week of August and can I be there for the orientation. I said of course I could be there and she said great, see you then. She seemed very nice on the phone, but when I hung up I was in shock. That was it, that was the interview, she really did not ask me anything about my teaching philosophy or how I would handle this position. All my preparation was not necessary, my nerves were so unnecessary as all she was looking for was someone who could come to her school and be licensed in front of a classroom. There was no concern with my true qualifications. She just knew I was a TFA corps member and I signed a two-year commitment, so she would not have to fill the position for at least two years.

The year I came to the school there were over 10 new teachers and it was very difficult to fill these positions within this rural community. The school established teams to support new teachers and the more seasoned teachers took their role of mentorship seriously. Yes, the hiring process was not that rigorous, but the support plan for the new teachers was robust and inspired and enriched my spark as a lifelong educator.

My first year teaching in New York City was at a small high school in downtown Brooklyn that had a strong program on law. I was hired as a teacher and the school's debate coach and when I came in, our senior team was the top team in the NYC Urban Debate League. I was told by the principal that the most important aspect of my job was to ensure they stayed as the number one team in New York. I honestly do not even remember the hiring process, but the previous debate coach was someone who judged me in numerous college debates and knew my debating skills. She was also at a point in her career where she did not want to coach the team anymore, but she was willing to train and support a new coach. I am sure that is what got me the job and I was at a time in my life where I was transitioning from North Carolina to live with my childhood friends in New York City. One thing I knew was that New York City was much more expensive than North Carolina and I could not move there without a job. As soon as I got the call from the principal that I got the job, all I needed was her letter of employment to take to the NYCDOE along with all my teaching credentials from North Carolina. I then applied for reciprocity and got into the NYC-DOE system, I was ecstatic. I was so thankful for the position as it got my foot in the door in the NYC Department of Education!

Finding My Home

In 2005, I began looking for a new school, and in New York City at the time large schools were being broken down into small theme-based schools. There were so many new schools opening and it was an overwhelming search as there were so many positions opening for the new school year. A friend of mine who also worked at my current school knew this was a great time to look for a new home and decided that a unique place to try and meet principals and learn about a school was to attend an eighth grade recruitment fair for incoming ninth graders. I remember being so nervous to enter this event. Here we were, two teachers holding our resumés while there were families running around to each school learning about what they had to offer. We definitely stuck out as we did not have an eighth grade child with us and we both looked extremely young, so I am sure there were principals looking at us with so much wonder. Are they eighth graders? Are they parents? Or wait, are they teachers looking for jobs?

But we did it. We went to each table, we asked a few questions to learn about the school, and then asked if they were hiring for the next year. When they said yes, we quickly gave our resumés. There was one table where we could not speak to the principal because he was so busy speaking with families. His table had so many students interested in speaking to him that there was no way we could get to him. We both were in awe of this school. We wondered what he was offering that was so different from the other schools, why does his table have three times the amount of people at it? Fortunately, before we left we were able to meet this principal, and he invited us to an open house at his school for educators. He told us the address, date, and time to be there. He said it will be informal, but we will have a chance to walk around the school building and meet with some students and current teachers to learn more about the school. My friend and I were both so excited and said we would definitely be there. I did not realize that this day walking around a fair I was not supposed to be at would change the rest of my life.

When we got to the open house, we were directed to the fourth floor and a student greeted us and told us they would take us on a tour and answer questions; when someone was ready to speak to us individually they would show us where to go. I was shocked to learn how small the school was. It was only half of the fourth floor and because the school was still growing, most rooms were not even in use. I cannot remember any of the questions I asked or what I learned about the school, but I do remember my friend went in first to speak to the staff members and she was in the room for maybe 10 minutes. This put me at ease as it was not a full interview, so when I walked in, I confidently put my backpack down, sat down, and was ready to go. There were two people in the room with me and I was sure they were both staff members. I did not learn that one of the people interviewing me was a student until the first day of school when there was a familiar face in my room. That "staff member" later told me I seemed so confident and she mentioned that I had a backpack in the interview rather than a professional bag. Who knew this bag would have this representation of confidence?

I will never forget at the end of the open house. The principal explained to us that the next step of the interview process would be for him or a staff member to visit our current school to see us teach. We were nervous and excited, but we were also not open with our current administration that we were looking for a new position. We asked that a staff member come to our school rather than the principal so our current administration would not be concerned with the visitor coming.

I do not remember the exact lesson I created for the demo, but I do remember the nerves and excitement I felt. We both told our students that someone was coming to observe us for graduate school and we hoped they would put their best foot forward for the lesson. The students in my school moved in cohorts, so they first had English and then they came upstairs to my class for history. The English classroom was a very large space, the teacher exuded more confidence than me in general, and she was extremely organized, which is not a trait I always had but is something I developed over time. I was definitely nervous we would be compared. My classroom was extremely small. It was originally a space for small group instruction and the year the space was given to me was the first time it was a full classroom. I honestly have no idea how I fit all the students in the room and how I managed to rotate around the classroom. The students sat at round tables, which at times was to my advantage because as long as I had a rich task, the students were able to talk and engage with each other, but at other times it was a complete distraction.

When my class before the demo left, my phone rang. It was my friend and she called to inform me that the students were extremely off. They would not stop talking and would not focus on the learning throughout her observation. Of course, this was the opposite of what I wanted to hear, as the class was entering into my space along with our guest observer. At first I was so nervous, but as soon as my students sat down and I handed out the "Do Now," I could tell my students were ready to participate and engage in the learning for the day. One student called me over to his desk and whispered, "You got this, Miss." I remember this so well because it showed me my students wanted me to be successful with this observation. They showed that they cared about me and from that moment on I knew the relationship and culture I built within this classroom would be something that stuck with me forever.

The interview process did not end with this demo. I was called back to the building for an in-depth interview with the Director of Programs and Partnerships and the principal. Then, after that interview, the school checked my references and offered me the position. When I was offered the job, I had to sit through one last interview. This interview was more of a formality at the time, but without it I could not be hired. I was interviewed by a committee of parents, teachers, students, administrators, and members of the teachers union to ensure I was the right fit for the school. It's not a coincidence that the school with the most purposeful approach to hiring is the one where I found my professional home and where I've spent the majority of my education career. This rigorous interview process showed me the value this school places on their teachers and it was under this principal that I grew as an educator and I am honored to lead this very same school today, my professional home for the past 18 years. I wake up every morning and head into the same building each day and find joy within my community. This allows me to continue to do the best I can for every student within my school.

Rebekah's Turn

Doing the Hiring

Although I was only a second-year teacher with very little experience in the system, my principal sent me to observe demo lessons by teachers applying for positions at our school. He wanted a sense of their teaching skills, and the teachers didn't want their current principal to know they were applying for other jobs, so the best cover was for another teacher to come for a visit. The school was in downtown Brooklyn, and I was supposed to visit the classrooms of two teachers who had previously attended an open house event during an earlier stage of the application process. Here's what I remember: the energy in those two classrooms could not have been more different, even though it was exactly the same group of students. I followed them to their English class and then to their social studies class. The English class was a place where sarcasm was the mother tongue. I don't remember the exact words anyone was using, just the energy of the memory I have left. It's pinched and snippy. There is no joy, love, or wonder in it. I knew we could not hire that teacher.

Then I followed those same students to their social studies class, which was in a small room that didn't seem to be originally intended for use as a classroom for 30 students. I sat at a small round table with a couple of students, and there was a large plant nearby. Half the lights were off, probably to mitigate the harsh fluorescent glow of institutional lighting. The lesson began; I don't remember anything about it, except for this: a student at my table was not on task. He was friendly and charismatic and engaged with me and his classmates. He swung his body around to look at his classmates and flung his limbs in their direction as he talked and laughed. The social studies teacher approached our table and stood next to him. She said his name and then she said, "I challenge you to write something down for number one."

That challenge was a spell. The student immediately picked up his pen and started writing. And I knew we had to hire that teacher. It was Meredith. But I would have never seen that interaction if Meredith had done her demo lesson at our school with our students, because what she said to that student was a reflection of the relationship she had built with him. She knew what to say to connect with and motivate him, and he trusted her and knew that her challenge was an opportunity, not a threat. I wanted that teacher to be my colleague.

While most of a teacher's day is spent with their students, in my experience the most important people you work with are your colleagues. These are the people who will inspire you, support you, challenge you, encourage you, make last-minute copies for you, let you borrow their laptop charger, surprise you with a candy bar, and join you at happy hour. Most importantly, these are the people who will help you achieve your purpose and remind you why you're doing this work when you're overwhelmed by all that makes it difficult. While you can't—and shouldn't—pick your students, you can sometimes pick your colleagues. For most of my teaching career, I belonged to a department of passionate, tireless, and driven educators who were in love with what they taught every day and wanted to engender that same love in our students.

So that's what I'm looking for in the hiring process: people who are in love with what they teach. They don't have to love *all* of it or every aspect of teaching it. But they need to feel genuine excitement, curiosity, and passion for what they teach, no matter what that content is. They should get a lot of fulfillment from geeking out about it. They should want to learn more about it for its own sake, not because they have to. They should want to do it in their spare time, whether that's reading books, touring museums, traveling to historically significant places, running marathons, making art, or anything else. Essentially, they should *want* to do the real work of their discipline. Otherwise, it's very hard to make their content come to life for their students.

Our department was a team of teachers in love with language and literature, and this was no accident. I played a significant role in hiring many of the teachers I worked with, both within and beyond my department. Some of them I knew through college or graduate school connections or had been my own students when I trained preservice teachers or worked as an adjunct instructor. Once they were hired, I mentored them if they were new to the profession, led the teams we belonged to, and served as an informal peer coach until that became one of my official job responsibilities as a teacher-leader. I knew my experience at school would be directly impacted by my relationships with my colleagues, and I was deeply invested in recruiting and supporting other teachers as a result. Many of us felt that way.

The opposite is true, too. There was one memorable demo lesson that Meredith and I and our principal and assistant principal once observed by a math teacher. Despite being in a classroom with a wall-length whiteboard and a functioning smart board, this teacher was scribbling equations on a tiny handheld whiteboard and then holding them up at close range in front of individual students to solve. It was bizarre and raised a red flag for me. It made no sense, even within the surreal and artificial context of a demo lesson in late June. Meredith and I were unimpressed, and we advised our school leaders not to hire this person. They did anyway, and the teacher lasted one year at our school, during which he repeatedly tried to intimidate students and other staff members. The invasion of students' personal space with his miniature whiteboard was a harbinger of his lack of boundaries and disrespect for others.

At the same time, letting the question "Who do we want to work with?" rule the hiring process meant that a lot of the teachers I worked with were like me; we had similar backgrounds, experiences, belief systems, and outlooks, which also meant that we had blind spots borne from our own ignorance and bias. For many years, we were a school where the leaders and most of the teachers were white, while nearly all of the students identified as BIPOC. Our desire to recruit colleagues we wanted to work with led us to assemble a faculty of people who were also like us—and not representative of our student body. Because justice, equity, diversity, and inclusion were not part of our school's purpose at the time, we did not prioritize these values in the hiring process, and our staff demographics did not reflect those of our students.

Aligning People, Positions, and Purpose

I struggled with burnout off and on for most of my last five years in the classroom, limping into June feeling depleted, ineffectual, and directionless. I dealt with my burnout in different ways, including looking for other jobs. Over those five years, I entertained many other professional possibilities, from teaching at another school to getting my administrative license to decamping for an instructional leadership position in a charter network. But I never followed through with any of those opportunities. I knew that the freedom and autonomy I enjoyed at my school, which are among my personal core values, would be difficult to find in other positions. Ultimately, I feared the changes I would face if I left my comfort zone, so I chose the environment that felt safe, even though I was increasingly unhappy there, over the risk of going somewhere new.

Instead of leaving, I kept finding ways to temporarily ward off the worst of my burnout and find ways to stay inspired and engaged in my work at my current school. I continuously promised myself that it would be for just one more year. Some years the most effective strategy I found was saying no to leading teams, mentoring first-year teachers, leading clubs, or doing anything else except for teaching. Other years it was the opposite: taking on even more. And this was certainly true for my work as a lead teacher alongside Meredith, when I had the best of both worlds; we taught three classes a day and spent the rest of our time mentoring and coaching colleagues and designing our school's professional learning program. This was work that fed my purpose of ensuring all learners (including adults) have access to joyful, vibrant, enchanting, empowering learning experiences.

But even that work—among the most empowering and fulfilling of my entire career—was not enough to keep my burnout at bay forever. Through the last month of that school year and into the summer, the emotional toll was unavoidable. I came to the realization that I had outgrown my school in its current iteration and needed to leave so I could continue learning.

Additionally, one of the enduring tensions of my career in education has been the choice between depth and breadth of impact. As a teacher at a small school for almost a decade, I had a deep impact in a relatively tiny community. I worked with a thousand or so students during that time and spearheaded initiatives that lasted beyond my time at the school, but there are over a million public school students and almost two thousand schools in New York City alone. My sense of purpose—ensuring all learners have access to joyful, vibrant, enchanting, empowering learning experiences—doesn't apply just to the ones who spent time in my classroom.

It was in the midst of that summer, in between fertility treatments, sobbing fits, and moving to a new apartment, that I was offered a position that aligned with my purpose. After turning down so many other opportunities, I decided to leave my school to become an instructional and teacher leadership coach with the central office, working with adults at schools all across New York City. And when, after four years, our team lost its funding, I chose to leave the public school system altogether because I could not find another job that was aligned with my purpose in the ways that mattered to me. Instead, I started my own company so I could do the work I wanted to do. I use my company's purpose—to challenge the educational status quo by boldly asking "What if?"—as a litmus test for professional decision-making about everything from what work I do to who my clients are to how I spend my time.

Your Turn

We've already spent quite a bit of time thinking about our personal sense of purpose, but organizations have purposes, too. This interplay between your individual purpose and that of the school or district where you work can be complicated, and if they're not aligned, it's very possible you'll experience burnout or other forms of job dissatisfaction. So, a key factor in combating burnout is making sure you're working in a community with a similar or complementary purpose to your own.

This alignment of purpose is important and foundational. However, we know that many educators have less control over where they work than their curriculum, instructional practices, and professional learning pursuits. We also know that reflecting on the alignment of your own purpose with that of your colleagues, supervisors, and community might spark uncomfortable realizations and difficult decisions, and we want to acknowledge there are not necessarily easy answers to the questions this chapter might catalyze for you.

If you're in a professional community that's at odds with your own sense of purpose, you are very likely to experience burnout. If you don't want to suffer (and probably cause your students, your colleagues, and your loved ones to suffer, too), you have four options:

1. Do nothing and suffer.

2. Change what you can about yourself: your mindset, attitude, feelings, schedule, priorities, etc.

3. Change what you can about your community using whatever influence you have.

4. Find a community that shares your purpose.

The following prompts and exercises will help you assess how aligned you and your current or potential school's purposes are and how to address any misalignment.

Reflecting on Purpose

Return to the purpose you articulated at the end of Chapter 1 and reconsider it through these lenses:

◆ Whether you're actively looking for a new job or considering your current one, is your personal purpose aligned with that of your school or organization?

◆ If yes, how do you know? Where are the strongest and weakest points of alignment? How do these two purposes complement each other? In what ways can your school's purpose challenge you to grow? In what ways can your

personal purpose challenge your school to grow? Are
there any potential challenges you can foresee and maybe
even forestall?

◆ If not, how do you know? What is within your locus of
control to change, either in yourself or at your school? If
you accept or keep this position, what might be the impact
of this misalignment on you, your loved ones, your
colleagues, and your students? Are there any points of
alignment you might be able to build on? Are there
like-minded colleagues with whom you can create your
own purposeful community?

People, Not Positions

Remember the point we've been emphasizing in this chapter:
schools are made of people, not positions. You can always
develop new skills and grow knowledge, but it's much harder to
shift mindsets, values, and belief systems.

◆ What matters most to you as a person and a professional?
What are your personal mission, vision, and core values?
What about your school's?

◆ What has been your experience in the hiring process as an
applicant, hiring committee member, and/or colleague?

◆ What has felt like the priority—people or positions—and
what have been the implications of that focus?

Because we think it's essential to prioritize people over
positions, we also believe the most valuable part of a demo
lesson (even—especially!—if it doesn't go well) is the debrief
afterward. It's a chance for the candidate and the hiring committee to explore evidence of student learning, process the
strengths and challenges of the learning experience, and identify
shifts that could enhance student learning even further. These
reflective conversations offer an invaluable chance to surface
mindsets, beliefs, and values in a real(ish) context that's more
authentic than the hypothetical scenarios that often comprise
interview questions. We think it's a red flag when a school or
candidate wants to skip a reflective opportunity during the
hiring process or demonstrates an inability to engage in
reflection.

When You Want to Be Hired

Too often the hiring process gives disproportionate power to prospective employers. Remember that while they're interviewing you, you're also interviewing them. A school that wants to hire you should make a case for why they're a great fit for you, so remember that you're also evaluating them. Be prepared with research and questions to help you figure out whether their purpose is aligned with your own, as well as the other criteria that's important to you. If you know this is the right place for you, think about how you can prove that to the hiring committee by focusing on alignment of purpose and how you can help the school realize its vision for success, not just for your content knowledge and teaching experience.

- What role have mission, vision, and/or core values played in the hiring process as you've experienced it? What have been the implications?

- What are you looking for in a new school community? What kind of community do you need right now to fulfill your purpose?

- How do you know that a school's purpose is a good match for your own?

- What do you need to see and hear to evaluate a school where you would like to be hired? What products or activities should be part of the hiring process?

- Does the school prioritize justice, equity, diversity, and inclusion? How do you know? Where do you see the evidence and impact of the school's commitment to anti-racism, or lack thereof?

See the Job Search Preparation Tool in the appendix and at https://www.wiley.com/go/educatingpassionpurpose for a reproducible resource using these prompts. You might also ask a colleague you know well and trust to complete it with you in mind to see what they envision as the right community for you.

Change Is Hard

As we said before, we know this chapter and these reflective questions might lead you to uncomfortable realizations and decisions about where you work and who you work with. Change can be very hard, especially for educators who love their students and feel a sense of loyalty, obligation, and responsibility to their school community. But if you know you are experiencing burnout because of where you work, and it is not within your power to make changes that will positively impact your well-being, then it's worth making a change that will allow you to stay in the profession and continue working on behalf of students.

Additional Considerations for Leaders

As a school leader, it is essential to invest in the people in your building and to make sure your staff feels appreciated, seen, and empowered especially when their own purposes align to your vision and mission. There are numerous ways to do this and, in this section, we discuss how you can use the hiring process to empower your current staff and begin the onboarding process for new members of your community. We hope you walk away with ideas on how to use your hiring process to empower, inspire, and grow your community based on your mission and vision.

Creating Space to Connect and Explore Identities

To best support your community, you need to create space for educators to reflect on their own identities and how their identities impact their work as educators. Additionally, leaders must have a clear, honest understanding of their own racial identity and how it has impacted their life and work as an educator and leader to effectively lead communities of educators engaged in that reflective work, too. Here are a few ideas for how to create an authentic space for this collective work:

◆ Open the conversation: start from your own experience and identify your race in the conversation to encourage your staff to speak about their race. This also helps you understand the impact your race has on your position in the school community. As the school leader, you want to model this reflective process for your staff.

◆ Read Glenn E. Singleton's book, *Courageous Conversations about Race*, and identify staff members to become trained facilitators so they can run discussions with your staff on a regular basis, such as a monthly meeting for all adults in the community.

Use the Preparing for Conversations about Equity resource in the appendix and at https://www.wiley.com/go/educatingpas sionpurpose for more prompts to support your community's anti-racism work and the closing section of Chapter 1 for more on asserting a schoolwide equity stance.

Knowing What You're Looking For

For many reasons, schools often are governed by a fear of scarcity. It can feel like there's never enough of anything, particularly time and copy paper, but also money, sometimes classrooms, often "good" teaching assignments, and so on. Consequently, there can be a lot of fear and acting out of desperation, especially in hiring: *We need a math teacher. Does this one have a pulse? Great, they're hired.* But if a school has a strong sense of purpose and the foundational convictions to activate it—a mission, a vision, core values, for example—that act as a litmus test for decision-making, then it's easier to stay true to what really matters: finding the right teacher for *your* students and school community. So, for example, if cultivating a joyful love of learning in students is a school's purpose, then during the hiring process that school is looking for candidates who exude, foster, and champion joy. Anyone who doesn't is not the right fit for their school.

It's essential that any school or organization looking to add new team members establish clear criteria for strong candidates and that these criteria be derived from the institution's purpose. These criteria should focus on the qualities you want and need in your community, not exclusively on grade or subject area openings, certification requirements, or years of experience. Those traits matter, of course, but when they are prioritized to the exclusion of purpose, you risk hiring candidates who check those boxes but won't necessarily be the right fit for your community on any deeper level. Remember, the hiring process is one component of a long-term strategy to cultivate a transformational learning community that benefits all students.

- What kinds of people does your community need right now to reach your vision for the future?

- How do your school's mission, vision, and core values support and align to your hiring criteria?

- How do you know a candidate's purpose is a good match for your school?

◆ What do you want candidates to learn and understand about your school during the hiring process? How can you ensure they do?

◆ What do you need to see and hear to evaluate a candidate? What products or activities should be part of the hiring process?

◆ To what extent do your faculty and staff reflect the identities, backgrounds, and experiences of your students? If there is a disconnect between the racial and ethnic identities of your students and your staff, what gets in the way of ensuring staff demographics are aligned with your students' demographics? What changes do you need to make to ensure you are prioritizing justice, equity, diversity, and inclusion in your hiring practices?

The Transformative Process

Hiring can be a very daunting and frustrating task, as schools and school leaders make decisions based on projected openings and budgets. This is why it is essential to make sure the process has a powerful impact on the current educators within your community so you do not feel as if you are wasting time. Here is one process that can help with this that is currently used at Meredith's school. We know you might not be able to do this exactly, but we hope it provides you with ideas and an example on how to design a hiring process that aligns with your purpose. We know the hiring process looks different depending on district policies, union contracts, and other local factors, so consider this as an example and think about which aspects you have control over and what you might be able to implement. Take what you can and adapt what you need to.

See the Planning Tool for a Sustainable Hiring Process in the appendix and at https://www.wiley.com/go/educatingpassion purpose for a planning checklist and suggested interview questions that may also be helpful.

1. Assemble the hiring committee.

2. Norm the committee on the school's values and mission.

3. Organize an open house.

4. Conduct demo lessons, debriefs, and interviews.

5. Solidify any next steps.

6. Hire the right person.

Here is how Meredith uses the hiring process to empower her current school community:

◆ **Assemble the hiring committee:** When Meredith puts together her hiring committee, she thinks about the teacher-leaders and teachers in whom she sees potential. She also thinks about the department that has the antici-pated openings and tries to select teachers from within that department. The number of teachers on the commit-tee is determined by the number of potential openings. When Meredith asks a teacher to be on the hiring commit-tee, she is showing the educators in her community that she values their opinion and wants them to have a say in the future of the school community. Meredith uses this opportunity to empower the educators who she wants to be deeply committed to the school community.

◆ **Norm the committee:** This is an excellent opportunity to get the committee together and discuss the values that are most important to them as educators. It gives you a chance to hear from your committee about the values that are important to them and is an excellent way to ensure your values are aligned. For example, the values Meredith looks for in a candidate are that they are reflective, open to feedback, believe in the importance of a culturally respon-sive curriculum, and see themselves as an anti-racist educator who will continue to work to break down structures in our education system that promote racist ideology. Having open conversations with a hiring committee about these values can be very powerful and can connect your committee to your community and you as a leader. Meredith always tries to create an open and honest space within her community and this is another opportunity to open up a discussion on values and mission. If you take the time to engage them in the conversation, it can be extremely powerful. You want the educators on your committee to be able to talk about the school community clearly to all candidates so they get a deep understanding of your community and that they are making an informed decision before accepting a position.

◆ **Organize an open house:** In many situations, school leaders get hundreds of resumés and it is very difficult to decipher which candidate is the best to bring in for a demo and interview based on a resumé alone. This is why an open house can be very powerful. It can be in-person or virtual depending on the location of the candidates and needs of your community. During the open house, the staff interviews each candidate for 15 minutes, using all the same questions. This is the first opportunity to see if the candidates connect to the school values and mission. After the 15-minute interview with a staff member, a student tours the candidate around the school community if the event is in-person. As a committee, Meredith sets up a way to get feedback from the students after the tours prior to bringing any candidate back for the next step. Then, the hiring committee meets to discuss the staff and students' opinions to then decide who will come back for the next stage of the interview process. This is another space where you can empower your hiring committee to make decisions and discuss the values you want to see in your educators. As well, depending on how many candidates you have anticipated attending the open house, you might need to invite more staff to interview candidates. When this happens, Meredith holds a short norming meeting prior to the open house.

◆ **Conduct the demo process:** Once candidates make it through the open house process, they are invited for a demo lesson, debrief, and interview. This process is extremely important for the candidate and your team. It is a time where you can talk with your teachers about instruction and because they do not have a relationship with the candidate, it can provide an opportunity to help your current staff grow while you find a new member for your community. It is a great way to see how your teachers think about instruction because they are free to give feedback on a lesson when they do not have a personal connection to the educator. Teachers should have an opportunity to discuss the strengths and areas of growth for the lesson, and you should use this time to push your current staff's thinking on the specific areas you want to help them grow in. Be specific with your staff so they know you are working to grow their pedagogical approaches.

◆ **Solidify next steps:** There are times when you can hire a staff member directly after the demo and interview and there are other times when you might want to bring them back for a planning session to see how they cocreate lesson material or so they can meet other stakeholders. Whatever the next step is, make sure you are thoughtful and go with your gut. There are certain positions that are very hard to fill so you do not want to lose a candidate, but if you are still unsure, it is worth it to take the time to be confident in your hire. It is also best to be transparent with your candidates, especially if you are interested in the candidate. You do not want them to accept another position because they are unsure that you are interested.

◆ **Hire the right person:** After your committee makes their recommendations, you speak to references and review your budget, hire the right person for your team.

This process is extremely long and time consuming, but it will help you ensure you bring the right candidate to your community. It also shows the candidate that you value their experience and take the hiring process very seriously, as we should within this profession. A few suggestions on how you can make this process effective for the candidate:

◆ Be transparent with the candidate about the process. Most candidates do not expect such a long process. It is important to be transparent, so they know what step they are on and how many more steps they have to go through.

◆ For the demo, we recommend giving the candidate a specific time frame, which is usually 20 minutes. When it comes to a topic for the demo, we recommend having the candidate bring in a lesson on something they love to teach. This will give you a strong sense of who they are as a teacher and how they plan. You should, of course, tell them what grade they will be teaching, but it is not as important that the students have a ton of prior knowledge. It is more important to see how the teacher plans.

◆ The debrief is sometimes more powerful than the demo. This is where you can see how the candidate reacts to feedback. Even if you think it is the most amazing lesson, give the candidate feedback so you can see how they take it.

◆ Make sure the candidate feels they are interviewing you and learning about your community just as you are learning about them.

Reflective Prompts for School Leaders

Here are a few additional questions that can help guide your thinking through this process:

◆ Does your hiring process empower your school community and uplift their voices as well as allow the time to further connect with your school's vision and mission?

◆ Does your hiring process have space for the team and the candidate to reflect and connect with the school's mission and vision?

◆ Is there an opportunity for the candidate to evaluate your mission, vision, and core values?

◆ What happens when a teacher turns out not to be a good fit for your school? What does the exit process look like?

Building a Bench

Beyond immediate hiring needs, it's important to have a long-term strategy for building a transformative learning community by thinking about how you're building a bench or pipeline of empowered, purpose-driven teachers who know your community and share your collective sense of purpose. We have both worked with many colleagues who started as paraprofessionals, teaching assistants, school aides, and even as our own students and are now amazing teachers and school leaders. The following questions can help you consider the potential teachers who are part of your community already and how to develop them as educators:

◆ Who is already on your nonteaching staff or in your community who could be a really great teacher?

◆ How can you support their development so they become the teachers your students need?

◆ What partnerships does your school have or could you develop that would allow you to continue building your teacher bench? For example, do you host student teachers from a local graduate school of education? Do their cooperating teachers view them as their future colleagues? Do cooperating teachers see it as their responsibility to acclimate their student teachers to your school's purpose? Are you positioning student teachers to join your faculty in the future?

Use the Staff Member Community Involvement Survey in the appendix and at https://www.wiley.com/go/educatingpassion purpose to help you identify and establish even more opportunities for educators to make connections and take on leadership roles across the school community.

Chapter 7

Nourishing Your Network

> "Having mentors, guides, and advocates has
> been extremely important throughout my
> journey. Believing in a student even when they
> don't believe in themselves is a powerful way to
> change someone's trajectory."
> —Michael, Class of 2008

If you're reading this book, you don't need us to tell you that
being an educator is too hard to do alone. It's vital you have a
group of people around you that you can turn to for support,
encouragement, and reinforcement when you start to lose sight
of your purpose. In the previous chapter, we focused on choosing where you work. In this chapter, we focus on who you work
with—the interpersonal relationships you choose to cultivate as
a network of support. Who do you need around you and in what
ways to stay true to your passion and purpose?

In addition to building a community of folx who support you,
it's also essential to think about who needs support *from* you. If
you're concerned about burnout, taking on additional responsibilities as a mentor, coach, or leader might feel like another drain
on your time and energy, but we've found that giving back to the
educational community is an investment in our profession that
benefits both the giver and the receiver. In other words, providing support to others isn't just a good deed or a way to recipro-
cate the support that others give you; it's actually a replenishing
experience that can spark a reminder about why you're passionate about doing this work in the first place.

Investing in the profession allows you to build the educational
community you want to be part of. We've already talked a lot in
this book about recognizing what's in your control and taking
responsibility for the changes you can make. Being an active
member of a professional community allows you to expand that

locus of control through the impact that you have on others. Together, you can solve problems and tackle challenges that are too daunting for one person acting alone.

What we reflect on in this chapter:

◆ The personal and professional networks that have sustained us throughout our careers.

◆ How we've intentionally cultivated relationships with mentors.

◆ What schools and leaders can do to help educators find the supportive communities they need.

What we hope you take away from this chapter:

◆ How to build a professional support network that helps you live and work in alignment with your purpose.

◆ How to self-advocate so you get what you need while avoiding counterproductive behaviors.

◆ Especially for leaders: how to holistically support teachers by nourishing your adult learning community.

Meredith's Turn

Being the Younger Sister to a True Inspiration

I am a true believer that relationships are the key to your success. If you surround yourself with people who motivate you and push you to be a better person, I believe you will be the best version of yourself and you will open up opportunities for yourself throughout your life.

For me, one person I have always looked up to in my life and who has always been there for me through any and every obstacle is my brother, Justin. Justin is three years older than me and I have so many memories of us together as kids, from when we pretend wrestled, watched wrestling on TV, night swims when we lived in California, sleepovers in each other's rooms when we got our first Cabbage Patch kids, and of course I have plenty of times when we did not get along. Through everything, he has been the person who believes in me and has taught me so much in life.

I followed my brother in so many ways throughout life. In high school, he was very involved in moot court, so of course I joined when I had the opportunity. He got a job at TCBY serving frozen yogurt, so as soon as I was old enough for a job, I applied and started working there. Whatever my brother did, I followed. I tried to convince myself that I needed to go to a different college, so when I started applying for schools, I was convinced I should go to the University of New Hampshire, because it reminded me of the University of Vermont where Justin attended but it was different. Then, when I was going through the application process, I realized that UNH did not have a school of education, so in the end I applied to UVM and became a Catamount, following my brother again. The best thing that happened to me was to be able to go to college with my brother. We were able to get dinners together and when I was down or depressed, he was there for me.

Even to this day, Mike (my husband) and Helen (my sister-in-law) joke that any time Justin or I are on the phone, it is with each other. There are so many mornings that when I get off the train, I call Justin as I am walking down the street before I enter my school building. These calls give me the energy and drive to continue to push myself to be the best leader and teacher. My brother has shown me how I need to value my true self and I show up each day to ensure my students are loved, supported, and valued in this same way.

Challenging Patriarchal Norms

I feel extremely fortunate to have a family who supports and pushes me to be the best version of myself and this means being present for my students and staff. I will never forget the day my husband, Mike, took me out for dinner and told me that he wanted to start a family and that maybe I should continue to teach for a few more years before thinking of getting into an administrative position so we can start a family. He is also the same man who left his full-time job as a sports video editor to go part time as a freelancer for the same company when I took on the principal position at my school. This allowed him to take on more of the responsibilities at home so I could focus more on my school community and know that our two boys, Max and Luke, are taken care of on nights I need to work late.

I am so thankful for the sacrifices Mike has made with his professional goals to support my dreams. Mike has allowed me to have balance and we often talk about how we know we are breaking social norms that exist in our patriarchal society. For example, Mike is the one who does the majority of the cleaning, cooking, school drop offs, homework help, and so much more. When we moved to our home in Baldwin, I will never forget Mike being so excited that he met a mom at the bus stop who told him all about a daycare for our younger son. He then called the daycare, toured it, and signed Luke up for the school. This mom at the bus stop later became one of my closest friends in Baldwin. And now there are many times Mike texts our son's friends' moms to ensure our kids could have playdates throughout the week. It is the love and support from Mike, Max, and Luke that continues to allow me to be the leader I am and for us to live our lives to the fullest.

The Power of Mentors Who Believe in You

I had a college professor during my sophomore year in college who saw something in me and helped me see my true potential. Throughout my four years at UVM I took two classes with Professor Kahn. The first class was where I went to the local middle school and tutored students after school. The class met once a week on campus and once a week at the middle school. This was the first opportunity I had to form a genuine learning relationship with a younger student and I did not know if I was a strong tutor or not. But Professor Kahn saw something in me and asked me to take another course with her and to be her teaching assistant (TA) in the course. This was a course where UVM students went to the same local middle school and taught middle school students how to tutor elementary students in supporting their reading and writing skills. As the TA, it was my job to ensure the middle school students were prepared and matched with an elementary student who they could support. I also paired the college student with a pair of middle school students to coach through the entire process. I remember having a feeling that Professor Kahn believed in me in ways my mother would've believed in me if she were alive. There was a sense about her and the way she made all her students feel so special that reminded me of my mother. She showed me my potential as a future educator and leader.

In my first two years in the classroom, I had two amazing mentors: Mrs. Walker, the mentor the district assigned to me, and Mrs. Fuller, the mentor I sought out myself. Both educators were amazing leaders, strong teachers, and women I admired in so many ways. They were both extremely different but I absorbed so much from the two of them. In my first two years of teaching, I knew I had a lot to learn. I was a new person with no experience and did not come from the community. I actually had never been in a town with just one traffic light, multiple churches, and trailer parks that were segregated by race. The knowledge and support I received from my mentors gave me a greater connection to the community and tremendously impacted my growth during my first two years of teaching.

When I left North Carolina and moved to New York City, I still sought out educators to learn from and the colleagues in my school knew I would come to them to ask questions or just talk about lessons. When I transitioned to my current school, I was very fortunate to work under an amazing leader, Lawrence. Whenever he came into my classroom and I had the opportunity to get feedback from him, I cherished it. A few things stuck with me and I still give this advice today when working with teachers. He told me to ensure I was aware of my physical presence within the classroom. When I called on a student, to make sure I would stand away from them, as this would get them to project their voice. He told me I needed to teach from all angles and points in a classroom. His office was also always open for me to talk about my upcoming history lessons. It was through his belief in me that I grew and I continue to emulate him as a leader today.

When I became an assistant principal, my principal Matt always expressed his confidence in me as a leader. He knew I had the desire and skills before I did, so he connected me with a leadership coach, Ken. Ken was one of the toughest mentors I have worked with, but I grew during the two years of working with him and what grew most was my confidence. When the work session with Ken would come to an end, my head would feel like it was palpitating as I left thinking so much about my leadership style and how I could have the greatest impact on my community. He also showed me that my instincts were those of an educational leader and that I had my dad's leadership skills deep within me. He showed me I could be a principal who turns around the school for success. He showed me that my instincts were ones of a principal and he helped me see what I had inside me to be the school leader.

Cultivating a Team and Helping Leaders Rise

As a principal, I have a team of educators and an administrative team that takes care of me, and having this team drives me to continue. Cultivating this team has been essential to ensure I am strong enough to lead the school each day and continually work to improve the education at my school. I also work hard to identify the passion within my team and ensure they are working in alignment to their purpose.

The school's payroll and purchasing secretary, Emmy, does so much more than any job description. Every morning, we check in on each other and make sure we are in the right mental and physical space to lead the school community. Each year, she pushes herself to grow and learn every single NYCDOE system so she can show up for our students and staff. Axel is a founding team member of our school community and when I started at the school, he was the dean of students. He continued his education to become a business manager. Our school is small and we do not have a business manager position, but I worked to create a space for him to shine within his expertise while filling a need for our community. Our data specialist, Jeff, and I got to share an office when I became the assistant principal. This was one of the greatest opportunities I had during my first year as an administrator. He taught me so many invaluable lessons from an administrative perspective and this helped me transition from a teacher to an assistant principal. When he went back to school and got his guidance counselor degree, it was an honor to be able to change his role within our community.

Now there are so many amazing colleagues that I can count on as a principal and these amazing educators uplift me and the entire school community. The key I have found is to know your people, know their strengths and passions, and make sure their work feeds it so they can be their best. My support list is long and changes each year but having my team is what supports me each day. We need to continue to invest in each other within the school community, as this profession is so challenging in many ways and you never want to feel alone. As two of my former students and now colleagues, Alvaro and Sabrina, wrote to me, "In order for a community to thrive, we must understand each other. This requires constant respect, communication and trust. Once you build that foundation, you're set up to form strong, long-lasting relationships."

My Teacher Champions

I have always been a people person and I have always turned to and leaned on people at times when I have been in need. I also always work to support others when I can. My friends and family were the ones who lifted me up when I was in some rough spaces throughout my high school years. This continued for me when I got to college; I developed very strong friendships and everyone who knew me in college also knew Sam. It was rare that we were ever apart. She was my other half in college and supported me throughout those four years and still today. She was the friend who helped me find therapy to help me address issues I needed to work on with losing my mom at such a young age and the friend who was beside me in numerous college adventures. There are so many people who have impacted my life and it is all the people who touch my life that make me who I am.

When it comes to teaching, it is no different. During my first two years in North Carolina, I relied on my TFA friends and roommates to help remind me of the importance of our work, and together we constantly reflected on how we could be better. I continued building relationships with teachers at every school I worked in. Tammy and I created a dynamic end-of-year project where the students connected every book they read to a historical event they learned in my class. She even helped me find my voice and always pushed me to not just say my ideas at happy hour with her but to bring them alive in the school.

I also met Anna, Rebekah, and Nina at my current school. Anna was in her first year when she started and I was in my third year. I remember that I was told I would be her mentor and our rooms were right next to each other. During Anna's first year, I tried to help her and mentor her but the reality was that there were so many more times when I came into her classroom needing her support than she came to mine. She and I both got into administration at similar times and are always there for each other.

Rebekah and I taught together at our school for eight years and we had the amazing opportunity to work together as lead teachers. During our time as teachers, we both had very different styles, but at the same time we both created relationships with our students that showed them how much we cared for them. I was always in awe of the high expectations Rebekah held in her classroom and I learned so much from her when we created professional development for the teachers in our school and became the mentors at our school. I learned how to organize myself in ways that would help not only push my practice but also the work my students produced.

I am also lucky to have worked with Nina for so many years. We taught together for many years and then I became her supervisor when I became the assistant principal and now principal of the school. She became a true friend of mine. Nina is the most passionate individual I have ever met and her passion and energy is contagious. When I need a pep talk or a thought partner, I know I can always count on Nina for an ear and advice. We have felt burned out together and we have worked together to overcome it and connect each other back to our students.

These are only a few of the friends and colleagues who have influenced me professionally and personally. If I wrote about everyone in my life, this could be an entire book, but the purpose here is to know that this profession is one where you dedicate yourself to it and you need to ensure you have a team there to support you. This team can be in your school or out of it but make sure they are helping you be true to yourself and your purpose.

Rebekah's Turn

Team You

After several years of struggling to get pregnant, I was diagnosed with stage 4 endometriosis in 2013. Unfortunately, Western medicine doesn't have a clear answer for what causes endometriosis or how to cure it, so I turned to other modalities for help. I worked with two acupuncturists, an Ayurvedic health coach, a physical therapist, a chiropractor, a Maya Abdominal Massage therapist, and numerous yoga teachers. I found a fitness instructor I loved, and I kept seeing my therapist. My partner referred to all of these people as Team Rebekah.

As an educator you need a Team You, a community of people who support you. The community that has supported me as an educator has changed over the past 20 years, and has included an evolving group of people, depending on where I was on my professional journey and what I needed at the time to help me stay true to my purpose. They've included people I learn *from*, like mentors, coaches, teachers, and therapists; people I learn *with*, like peers, colleagues, friends, and collaborators; and people I *teach*, like mentees, coachees, employees, and students. (This framing of my professional community has been informed by Tai Lopez's "law of 33%.")[1] And because I've known some of these people for two decades, my relationship to them has changed, and they've switched categories. For example, when I first met Rachel, she was a first-year teacher and I was her mentor. But since then she's become one of my closest friends, collaborators, and professional partners. For many years now, I have seen her as someone I learn alongside, not as the first-year teacher I mentored so long ago. And I'll bet some of my own mentors see me as a peer now, too.

Who I Learn From

My first teacher mentor, way back before I even thought about becoming a teacher, was Ms. Leone, my eleventh grade English teacher and twelfth grade creative writing teacher. Ms. Leone's real-world writing assignment resulted in "Cuento de Cucumber," the short story I wrote from the perspective of a cucumber after seeing a truck full of them outside my school and that my Harvard interviewer asked me to read aloud after I told her I loved writing. Ms. Leone sparked the love of literature that is still with me today and showed me what it looks like to teach from that love with the goal of engendering it in your students, too. Almost 30 years later, when I read the poem "Recuerdo" by Edna St. Vincent Millay today, I picture Ms. Leone raising her upturned fist while reading the line, "And the sun rose dripping, a bucketful of gold." Because of Ms. Leone, I took my students back and forth on the Staten Island Ferry while we read that poem together. As a high school student, I didn't know that I wanted to be a teacher, but I knew I wanted to be like Ms. Leone.

Ms. Leone treated us like young adults, not kids. It wasn't just that she sent us out into downtown Miami to find something to write about. It was also the kind of literature that she shared with us. In her class we read Charles Bukowski and Zora Neale Hurston, and when we read William Carlos Williams we didn't just read "The Red Wheelbarrow" like everyone else; we read "This is Just to Say," and all our minds were blown. I wanted to be a teacher who blew students' minds, too, who showed them new ways to think by giving them new things to read. Ms. Leone's classroom enchanted me by casting a lifelong spell, and that's what I want for all learners I work with, too.

Once I actually became a teacher, I was fortunate to work with mentors, coaches, and guides who inspired me as a learner and an educator. My first officially assigned mentor, Carolyn, taught me everything from how to design handouts on half sheets of paper, because our school only allowed us to make 1,500 copies each semester for our 150 students, to how to deal with the veteran teacher who yelled at me in the teacher's lounge. Another mentor, Kristen, once visited my class and watched me teach the same lesson three times in a row. When we debriefed after that final class, she showed me her notes with the exact words I'd used to explain the lesson's key concept, and I realized that I had used different phrasing each time. This explained why I'd seen different learning outcomes from my students in those three classes. I had no idea I was explaining things in different ways, but she had held up a mirror that allowed me to see my teaching practice from a vantage point that was otherwise inaccessible to me. Years later, when I became a coach myself, I often thought about the gift of self-sight Kristen gave me that day, and I tried to do the same for the teachers I supported. Another coach, Alexis, spotting the stricken look on my face after a particularly frustrating day as a lead teacher, took me down the hallway so we were out of earshot, and said, "You want to change minds to change practice. But sometimes you have to change practice to change minds." Her words have stuck with me for the past decade as I've continued to think about what it takes to transform schools and classrooms.

When I was growing up, I thought that therapy was for people who were sick or had experienced indelibly traumatic events. This is not true. Having a trained professional to talk to who is outside of my personal life, with no vested interest in the choices I make or the actions I take, whose sole job is to help me figure out how I feel, how I want to feel, and what I can do about it, has impacted all facets of my life, including my work as an educator. If you are committed to maintaining your resilience as an educator and have never been in therapy, it may be something to consider. You do not need to be in the throes of a crisis to start therapy; rather, therapy can actually help you ward off those potential crises, including burnout, by giving you the tools to live a life aligned with your purpose.

Who I Learn With

In addition to the teachers, mentors, and coaches I learn from, I've also cultivated a community that includes peers: educators at a similar point in their professional and personal lives as me. With these friends and colleagues I share a common lexicon, and they are people I often turn to when I want to bounce ideas around about teaching and learning.

For example, as a member of a district-level team of instructional and teacher leadership coaches working with schools across New York City I experienced the best professional development of my life. Nearly everything I know today about coaching and facilitation I learned from my manager and colleagues on that team and the external training experiences I had access to. I learned how to hold up a mirror for other educators, just as Kristen and Alexis had done for me. As a classroom teacher, I had often thought of myself as a lone wolf, but as a Teacher Development Coach (TDC), I learned to collaborate, share, and listen. And when things went sideways and I made mistakes or wasn't sure what to do, my fellow TDCs were there to help me debrief, reflect, and even role-play what I would do differently next time.

Who I Teach

At the same time, as a TDC, I learned so much from the teachers I coached that I often ruminated about returning to the classroom because I knew I would be a much better teacher after having been a coach. Seeing myself and my teaching practice reflected in the teachers I worked with allowed me to understand myself more clearly and to see where I had gone wrong and what I could do better. Visiting classrooms and experiencing teaching practice from the students' perspective taught me more about how learning works than any graduate course or PD workshop ever did.

I've also taken these lessons about supporting others and the way their growth reinforces my own sense of purpose into my work beyond the education system. As a small business owner, I've struggled to find a balance between the work I want to do and the work that needs to be done. Ultimately, what's been helpful to me is to understand that I don't need to do everything—and I can't. Not only do I not have the physical resources to do it all without burning out, I can't stay true to my purpose if I'm diffusing my energy, ideas, and creativity across too many causes and concerns. I have a more significant impact when I concentrate my resources on projects and activities that are aligned with what really matters to me and what I'm actually good at. What about all the other things that still need to get done? That's where it's been essential that I understand my job as a leader: to support my employees in identifying the work they love and are really good at and to empower them to take leadership roles where they can succeed.

Your Turn

People plus Purpose

Return to the purpose you articulated at the end of Chapter 1 and reconsider it through these lenses:

◆ Who helps you fuel your purpose? How do they support you?

◆ Who hinders your purpose? How do they get in the way of your *why*?

◆ Who do you know who shares your purpose or whose purpose complements your own?

◆ If you could bring anyone, living or dead, into your network to help you fulfill your purpose, who would it be? Why?

◆ Who could you realistically invite into your network? What might that invitation look like? What would you hope to gain from building a relationship with them?

A Framework for Thinking about Your Network

In the TEDx Talks "Why I read a book a day (and why you should too): The law of 33%," Tai Lopez shares a framework for thinking about professional networks as composed of three groups of people:[2]

1. Those you look up to for inspiration and guidance because they have more experience or success than you (mentors, coaches, teachers).

2. Those who have the same level of experience and success as you (friends, teammates, co-teachers, happy hour buddies).

3. Those who look up to you for inspiration and guidance because you have more experience or success than them (mentees, coachees, student teachers, graduate students, preservice teachers, people who are considering becoming teachers, students, newer colleagues, first-year teachers).

If this framework resonates with you, make a list of all the people in your professional community and sort them into one of these categories. Keep in mind that some people may have switched categories over time (as when a mentor becomes a peer, for example). Once you've created your lists, consider the following questions:

◆ What do you notice about your lists?

◆ Does anything surprise you? What does looking at your community through this framework help you see that you might have been unaware of?

◆ Are your lists fairly balanced, or do you have more people in some categories than others? Why do you think that is? What might have led you to have more mentors than mentees, for example?

◆ Consider your current relationship to burnout. Do you see any connections between how you feel and the professional community you've cultivated? For example, are you at a point in your career where you need mentors who can help you explore new models for teaching and learning? Have you found a way to sustainably maintain your investment in the profession and want to share what you've learned with early-career teachers? Are you yearning for new teacher friends?

◆ What actions does this framework inspire you to take? How would you like to grow your professional network so it provides the nourishment you need right now?

See the Network Reflection Tool in the appendix and at https://www.wiley.com/go/educatingpassionpurpose for a reproducible resource you can use to assess your professional network. We especially recommend using this tool to identify the folx you want to periodically thank or reach out to in case they're in need of support.

Beware of (Only) Venting

We know from personal experience that one thing educators often do when they gather together is vent. Venting can feel good in the moment, especially when you see your concerns and frustrations reflected back to you by your colleagues. But when the conversation never moves forward from venting, it can be destructive. If venting to your colleagues is your only outlet for expressing your emotions, you might be inadvertently feeding your burnout. Here are some strategies to ensure that venting doesn't turn toxic:

◆ Identify ways to express your emotions beyond venting to your teacher friends. Strategies like journaling, doodling, exercising, calling a friend or family member in a different profession, pouring your feelings out in a voice memo, and talking to a therapist can provide you with emotional outlets that allow you to express how you feel without getting stuck in a negative spiral with others who feed off of your emotions and vice versa.

◆ When you need to vent, set a timer and stick to it. Breathe all the fire you want, but when the timer goes off, move on to another topic or a different way of talking about what's bothering you.

◆ Make happy hour a no-venting zone. Institute a similar norm for team meetings: the first person to vent has to bring the snacks next time.

◆ Transition the conversation from venting to solutions by focusing on where you can have a meaningful impact. Remember, you can't control other people, only yourself. What can you realistically change to make the situation better for you and, most importantly, your students?

What If You're Having Trouble Finding Mentors?

Traditionally, mentors have been defined as people who must be older, wiser, and more experienced than us, but we like to think of them simply as people, including peers, we can learn from. If you haven't found the right mentor for you yet, see if reframing what a mentor is in this way helps you broaden your potential pool of mentors. Mentors don't have to be older than you or have been teaching longer than you. It's true that they generally have areas of expertise that you're hoping to learn from, but that doesn't mean they have to be an expert in absolutely every growth area you've identified. Who do you know who seems to have mastered or achieved a level of success in something you aspire to? It might also be helpful to look beyond your own context for potential mentors; there could be someone with experience in a different grade, subject, or specialization who might be a resource for you. For more resources on how to cultivate effective mentoring relationships, see Chapter 7 as well as the Mentor Matching and Reflection Tool in the appendix and at https://www.wiley.com/go/educatingpassionpurpose.

Additional Considerations for Leaders

Everything we've said in this chapter about the importance of nourishing a professional network applies to leaders, too. If you're the head of a school or district, you also need a chosen community of people who challenge, support, and learn from you.

Supporting Teachers Through Community

We've noticed a growing awareness over the past couple of years about the importance of teacher wellness and the need for schools to support teachers in prioritizing self-care. We believe true self-care means living and working in alignment with one's purpose, not surface-level solutions like meditating at the beginning of meetings, staff yoga breaks, or doughnuts in the teachers' lounge. Making a career in education sustainable requires structural changes and, depending on your leadership role, you may or may not be able to meaningfully impact those structures, like ensuring the class schedule provides teachers with regular breaks for personal needs, the ability to go to a doctor's appointment during regular business hours, and planning periods for ongoing collaboration with colleagues. Either way, all leaders can support the educators they supervise in building relationships that will nourish them. For example, many teachers have mentors during the first year in the classroom. Far fewer mid-career teachers have mentors or coaches with whom they meet during the school day. As a leader, how can you create space to understand what your staff needs? What rituals or routines can you champion to ensure everyone on your staff has a network, not just first-year teachers?

We believe it's also a leader's responsibility to monitor team members for potential signs of burnout and to intervene when necessary. (See Chapter 2 for a reminder about burnout indicators and risk factors.) If you suspect a staff member is struggling or operating in a way that's not sustainable, for the good of your students you need to be prepared to have a candid conversation with them about the support they need and the changes that will help them move forward. A blunt conversation about sustainability with a school leader might have helped Rebekah when she was in the throes of burnout. In contrast, as a principal Meredith has had countless conversations with teachers about how to deal with burnout. These are not always the most comfortable conversations for either party, but they are necessary.

Make Coaching a Priority

When a leader prioritizes coaching for all members of their team, they are telling the community that this is first and foremost a learning community. And isn't that what a school is? This belief starts at the top: as a leader you should have a coach, and your team should see you protecting time to meet with them and understand what you're working on with your coach (with as much transparency as your comfort dictates). Everyone on your staff—not just teachers—should give and receive feedback grounded in trusting relationships with colleagues, mentors, and coaches who are adequately trained. Too often it's assumed that educators who are good at their job will be good at coaching others to do that job. However, coaching is a separate skill set in itself, and it has to be learned. Being a good teacher doesn't mean you can automatically coach other teachers effectively. Coaches and mentors need training, development, and support.

The Staff Lounge

Many schools have a dedicated space for staff to gather outside of classrooms and offices, but these spaces are not always designed with a clear purpose in mind, which can cause disagreements about how the space should be used and even contribute to a toxic environment of gossip and excessive venting. If you are a decision maker about space use in your community, you should have a clear vision for how a staff lounge or other adult gathering space will be used, and that purpose should be cocreated with the staff members who will use it. An intentionally designed staff lounge can be a productive, inclusive environment where all staff go to not simply take a break and complain but to work through whatever they need at the time. As a leader, you have an opportunity to design this space thoughtfully so its purpose is clear and it supports growth in your community. These questions can help you reflect on the relationship between purpose and design in your staff lounge.

The Reflecting on Community Spaces for Collaboration resource in the appendix and at https://www.wiley.com/go/educatingpassionpurpose provides additional prompts to support purposeful staff lounge design and use. You might distribute a version of this resource to your staff as a survey to elicit their input about how the staff lounge should be designed and used.

- ◆ How do you and your staff want the space to be used? Is it for hanging out and socializing? Is it for collaborative work? Is it for lunch and birthday celebrations? Is it for professional learning? Get clear on the space's purpose and ensure you and your staff have a shared vision for how it will be used.

- ◆ Where is the space located? Does it feel like an extension of an administrative or supervisory office, or is it a place where staff members can feel a sense of autonomy?

- ◆ What furniture is in the space and how is it arranged? If the purpose of the space is for learning or collaboration, are desks and tables arranged to support that kind of work? If the space is for hanging out and eating lunch, are there couches and comfortable chairs that invite lounging and collegiality?

- ◆ What resources do staff members need in the space? If this is where the copy machines are located, who ensures they are always stocked with enough paper? Is there signage to help users troubleshoot issues with copy machines, computers, or printers, and directions for who to contact for assistance? Is this where staff members can find classroom supplies or is that a separate space?

- ◆ Are there adequate spaces for clean food storage? Does the school provide snacks and beverages? What are the expectations for maintaining the refrigerator?

- ◆ What do staff members see when they are in the space? Are there reminders of the school's mission and vision? Are they surrounded by positive messaging? Are there pictures that celebrate the school community? What about student work, teacher work, and quotes from students and staff?

Notes

1. Lopez, T. (2015). Why I read a book a day (and why you should too): the law of 33%. TEDx Talks (15 January). https://youtube/7bB_fVDlvhc (accessed 25 November 2022).
2. Ibid.

Conclusion

"Students are like sponges, they absorb what
they see. The voices they hear from an authori-
tative figure become the voices in their head as
they are growing up."

—Edward, Class of 2009

The process of identifying one's purpose and connecting it to all
that you do in education is not an easy process. Educators get
into this field to make a difference in the lives of their students
and community. This profession takes a lot out of anyone who
dedicates themselves to it. There are so many obstacles that can
get in our way from doing the work we're passionate about.
We can let those obstacles be part of our defeat or we can take
time to learn from them, make the necessary changes, and push
through. How we push through and grow is up to us and
rooting yourself back to your purpose can always be a centering
place. In reading this book, we hope our stories helped you
connect to your own stories and purpose and think about what
you can control to be the educator your students need and that
you set out to be. Take care of yourself so you can continue to
work each day to transform the education system and promote
equity and justice for all students.

Remember, you must give yourself time to reflect, engage
with your feelings, and understand the root of burnout so you
can work to address it. There is so much power in listening to
your students, colleagues, friends, family, and inner voice when
you feel like you've lost your connection to your passion
and purpose.

The journey of writing this book has taken years, and even
though we conceptualized it when we were teachers, neither of
us is in the classroom anymore, but we are both working to
impact individual educators and the system at large in different
ways. We work every day to stay connected to our sense of
purpose. When we struggle and see the early signs of burnout
arising, we connect to these roots to build us up again. In our
final stories, we reflect on where we are now and how we
continue to keep our fires going.

Meredith's Turn

The School Leader Within Me

Throughout my life, I always thought I would be a teacher. When I was in college studying education, I never thought I would become a principal. I thought I would retire as a lifelong teacher. Then, during my last year as a classroom teacher, I was a lead teacher and was given the opportunity to run professional development, mentor teachers, and sit on the school leadership team, making more of a global impact on the school.

I will never forget when the assistant principal at the time told me he was looking for a new position and if he got a new job, I should consider applying for the assistant principal position at the school. What I realized at the end of that school year was that I owed it to myself to take on this leadership position and because I had such a deep knowledge of the school I should take this opportunity to try and make substantial change within the community. I remember being out at the end-of-year happy hour thinking that this could be my last time with my colleagues as a teacher. It was then that a fellow staff member who did not know about the movement of our assistant principal came right up to me and said he knew I was going to lead the school in the near future and he would be honored to work with me. I then received a personal text from the assistant principal that he had accepted a new position and would be letting the staff know the next day. I knew that all of these things were meant to be for me in my leadership journey and I needed to take on these opportunities. Even as an assistant principal, I kept thinking, "Wow, I am not going to become a principal," but as I developed, I knew that to have the impact I had the drive for I needed to take on this next step in my professional journey.

Throughout my years as an assistant principal, I would think about being the principal and I was never confident I was ready for the task. What I realize now is that no one is ever ready for such an intense position within education. Being the principal puts a lot of pressure on an individual to ensure everyone within the school community is working toward the betterment of every single student who walks through the school building. There is no issue that is not of your concern or that it is not your job to fix. This pressure is a huge challenge and yet on days when I struggle the most, I think about the stories of the individual students who push me to be better. It is

their voices and their drive that push me to be the leader
I am today.

Rebekah's Turn

Why I Left

I fear that the elephant in the room of this book has been my own
decision to first leave the classroom and then to leave the public
school system to start my own business. Over the past few years
while Meredith and I have worked on this book, I've worried
often that our readers would distrust me or doubt my credibility
on how to avoid burnout. When telling other members of my
professional community about this book, I sometimes found
myself apologizing or explaining why I felt like I had any right
to speak on this topic. What could I possibly teach others about
avoiding burnout when I had seemingly failed at doing so
for myself?

It was in one of these apologetic moments of self-doubt about
supporting teachers through burnout that my former coach
Alexis said to me, "But you didn't burn out on teaching. You
burned out on your school." Even though Alexis had long since
moved from being my coach to being my peer and friend, she
was still holding up the mirror. In an instant, I saw something
about myself that I had not seen before.

When I left my school to become a district-level coach in 2013,
it wasn't because I was burnt out on teaching. It was because I
didn't think I could continue to learn and grow in alignment
with my purpose at that school. I probably could have gone to
lots of other places to address that, including other schools, but
that was also the summer when I was undergoing fertility
treatments and preparing for surgery to try to figure out why I
wasn't getting pregnant. When the district coaching position
presented itself, I seized it because it seemed like a relatively
quick and easy way to change what I thought was missing from
my life at my school.

Later, when I resigned from the district in 2017, it wasn't
because I was burnt out on working in public education. It was
because there was no more funding for the coaching team I was
on, and bureaucratic credentialing rules prevented me from
switching to a different team. I could have returned to a classroom position or become a school-based coach, but I felt such a
strong and renewed sense of purpose from the particular type of

coaching I'd been doing for four years that I wanted to keep doing it, even if that meant becoming a freelance coach and doing it on my own, from outside of the public system.

Where We Go from Here

Alexis's mirror helped me see that I didn't leave because of burnout. I left, first my school and then the district, to *avoid* burnout. I left so I could continue working in alignment with my purpose because I didn't think it was possible to continue doing so where I was. Now I work for myself, running a business that is part unconventional children's bookstore and part educational consulting firm. I get to work with partners that have included educators, schools, leaders, parents, community groups, nonprofits, government agencies, public parks, family shelters, and other small businesses to help transform what learning and literacy look like in our education system and our society. I have no regrets about leaving the classroom or the district, but there are still things I miss and things I wish I could do that aren't possible anymore. It's a little like the decision my partner and I ultimately made not to have children: we are 100% confident we made the right choice, but we still think wistfully about what our lives might be like if we'd chosen the other path. I think of them as my shadow lives, the grayed-out versions of my story that are always trailing me, even when I can't see them.

It's sometimes treated like a tragedy when a public educator leaves the system, but I think that attitude is worth reconsidering. Ultimately, all students are our students, not just the ones at our individual school or even in our district or city. If inspired, purpose-driven educators want to continue to work on behalf of students, but feel they can no longer do so within a particular system or bureaucracy, that is not a tragedy. That is an opportunity. It's a chance to continue building an educational ecosystem that supports all students *and* educators, but seizing that opportunity requires reflection about why the current system is not working for those educators. In this book, we've focused on what individual teachers and the leaders who support them can do to avoid and heal burnout because that's where Meredith and I feel we can be most effective. But for readers who do have power at the district, state, and national levels, I want to acknowledge that there are systemic changes that are needed to transform this profession into one that does not treat burnout like an expected occupational hazard. If we want educators to continue to feel purpose - driven in their work, then the profession needs to change, not just the professionals.

Your Turn

Where Do You Go from Here?

Write a letter to your future self. What is your purpose right now? What are your hopes and fears about living and working in alignment with your *why*? Use the reflective writing you've done throughout the course of this book to compose this letter. Alternatively, go back to a specific chapter that resonated with you and dive deeply into those prompts and activities.

Seal the letter in an envelope with your address and a Forever stamp and give it to someone you trust. Ask them to mail it to you in five years. Having done this activity ourselves and with students, we know how powerful it can be to visualize your future and learn from your past. It's never too early or too late to recommit to your purpose.

Appendix

Reproducibles

Beginning of the Year Teacher Reflection Tool

One way to help teachers connect to their purpose and to why they became educators is to integrate reflection at the beginning of the year in your opening meeting. This tool is here to help educators connect their purpose to their professional goals for the year. This tool also can be used with a partner or coach who asks the prompts and then records what they hear. See Chapter 1 for more resources on articulating and exploring your purpose.

Why did you decide to become an educator?	
What inspires you to continue to be an educator? (This can be a person, a life event, etc.)	
What led you to be an educator in our school community?	
Describe your greatest success in the classroom from last school year. How did it impact student achievement?	
What pedagogical approach do you want to focus on for this year to improve instruction in your classroom?	
What is your goal for this year in regard to student achievement?	
In what ways do you hope to impact the school community this year?	
What support do you need or hope for this year?	

Burnout Self-Assessment Checklist

Are you experiencing burnout? Review this burnout checklist adapted from the Mayo Clinic[1] and mark the questions that you answer "yes" to. For every "yes," write down a specific example beneath that item that captures your experience. For example, if you answered "yes" to the first question, write down something specific that you said or thought that captures your cynical or critical feelings about your work. See Chapter 2 for more resources on identifying and addressing burnout.

◆ Have you become cynical or critical at work?

◆ Do you drag yourself to school and have trouble getting started with your day?

◆ Have you become irritable or impatient with colleagues, supervisors, students, or families?

◆ Do you find yourself blaming your students if they are not meeting your classroom expectations or lack motivation?

◆ Do you lack the energy to be consistently productive and engaging with your students?

◆ Do you find it hard to concentrate or focus both during and outside of work?

◆ Do you lack satisfaction from your achievements as a teacher and from those of your students?

◆ Do you feel disillusioned about your work as an educator?

◆ Are you using food, drugs, or alcohol to feel better or to simply not feel at all?

◆ Have your sleep habits changed?

◆ Are you troubled by unexplained headaches, stomach or bowel problems, or other physical complaints?

◆ Do you find yourself getting angry at things you cannot control?

◆ Have you found yourself doing things at work that you could have never imagined in the past?

The Burnout Spectrum

Where Are You?

No one wakes up one morning to discover themselves suddenly burnt out with no previous signs or warnings. Instead, the process happens gradually, over time, and then a sudden wake-up call alerts them (or their family, colleagues, or supervisor) to the crisis. We know everyone's experience with burnout is somewhat unique, so we created a Burnout Spectrum to capture what that gradual process can look like. See Chapter 2 for more self-assessment resources on burnout.

- ◆ Where on the Burnout Spectrum would you place yourself or the teachers you supervise right now? Mark that place on the spectrum.

- ◆ Do other stages of the Burnout Spectrum resonate with you? Annotate the spectrum to capture your past experiences. You might write a few notes or sketch an image.

- ◆ Think about the colleagues you know well. Do you see their experiences reflected on the Burnout Spectrum? What have you seen or heard from them that helps you to understand their experience?

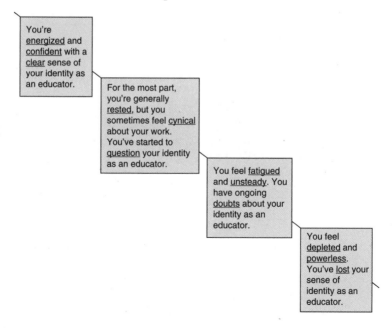

Connecting Schoolwide Policies to Your Purpose

When setting up your classroom system and structures, it is important to think about your purpose and the schoolwide policies that already exist. It is important that these systems and structures are aligned to your beliefs as an educator so you can enforce them and that they are consistent with all school policies. When the two conflict, it is very difficult for the educator to enforce the policy. This reflection tool is designed to help you work through this and also can be used to connect schoolwide policies to a school's own purpose. See Chapter 4 for more resources on purposeful policy design and implementation.

Use this reflection tool to plan implementation of schoolwide policies, potentially including but not limited to:

◆ Bathroom

◆ Homework

◆ Grading

◆ Electronics

◆ Lateness to class

◆ Attendance to class

◆ Birthday celebrations

◆ Visitors to your classroom

Insert the Schoolwide Policy Here:		
What is the relationship between your purpose as an educator and this policy?	How can you align implementation of this policy to your purpose?	How will you inform your students and families of this policy?
Do you have any concerns in regard to this policy in your classroom?		
What support will you need to implement this policy in your classroom with integrity?		

Excavating Your *Why* Reflection Tool

Spend some time journaling or drawing in response to any or all of these prompts to start uncovering your sense of purpose. These prompts also work well individually as icebreakers or opening activities at meetings or workshops because they allow educators to get to know each other in new ways. Even though you see your colleagues every day, you might never have spoken with them about these topics, and having these conversations can build relationships and a sense of community around a shared purpose. See Chapter 1 for more prompts and activities to help you uncover your *why*.

◆ How did you feel about school as a child?

◆ Who and what are the touchstones of your early experiences in school?

◆ What was your childhood perception of what a teacher did?

◆ What roles do teaching and learning play in your ancestry and heritage?

◆ How did your family influence you as a student and/or teacher?

◆ What sparked your interest in becoming an educator?

◆ When did you first realize you wanted to be a teacher?

◆ How did you become an educator?

◆ Why did you become an educator?

◆ Why do you stay an educator?

◆ What is in the soil where the roots of your teaching career took hold?

◆ If you are not a classroom teacher, how do you think about your role as an educator?

Fire Visualization Tool

Close your eyes and picture a controlled, purposeful fire, such as a backyard fire pit or a summer campfire. Imagine that this fire represents your professional capacity as an educator. The longer the fire burns, the more effective and enduring your career. If the fire burns too strong and hot, it might become uncontrollable or use up all of the available wood necessary to keep it going long-term. If it doesn't burn strongly enough, though, it will peter out or not be hot enough to keep you warm.

These prompts also work well individually as icebreakers or opening activities at meetings or workshops because they allow educators to get to know each other in new ways. Even though you see your colleagues every day, you might never have spoken with them through the lens of a metaphor like your professional fire, and having these conversations can build relationships and a sense of community around a shared experience. See Chapter 2 for more prompts and activities on identifying and addressing burnout.

Draw your fire below or paste an image that captures what it looks like.

Pull the threads of this metaphor:

◆ If your teaching career is a fire you're trying to maintain, what is the fuel you're burning to do so?

◆ What keeps your fire going?

◆ How long has your fire been burning?

◆ How strong is your flame right now?

◆ Are you using solid, healthy firewood, or twigs and scraps of paper you found lying around?

◆ What happens as your fire burns?

◆ Is there more fuel at the ready or are you scrambling for something else to keep your fire going?

◆ How do you know when the fire is winding down?

◆ Are you constantly monitoring its state or are you caught off guard when the flame gets low?

◆ Do you want your existing fire to burn continuously or is it necessary to scorch the earth and build a new fire?

◆ What's in the ashes created by your fire?

◆ Allow yourself to sit with this visualization and consider the metaphor from all angles. Notice what rises to the surface for you and feel free to journal about your insights and takeaways:

The Five Whys

One writer and thinker who has influenced our understanding of purpose is Priya Parker. Parker is a conflict resolution facilitator, and her book, *The Art of Gathering,* is a powerful argument for changing the way we come together in community, including in schools and classrooms. From Parker's work we've learned to use a protocol called The Five Whys. While Parker employs this protocol for uncovering the purpose of a gathering, we have used it for other purposes, too, and we think it's a great tool for understanding your personal *why*.

You can find lots of versions of this protocol online, but we designed this tool and the accompanying example especially for use with Chapter 1. In addition to using this tool to uncover your individual purpose as an educator, we've also used it to articulate the purpose of teams, events, and meetings, including occasions like holiday celebrations. For collective purposes, try having all participants answer The Five Whys on their own and then share their responses with each other to see where there are connections and distinctions. Reflect on what these overlapping and divergent purposes may mean for your community or event.

1. Why are you an educator?

2. Why?

3. Why?

4. Why?

5. Why?

6. Why?

7. Why are you an educator?

The Five Whys: Example

1. Why are you an educator?

To help prepare my students for the future.

2. Why?

So they can be successful as they get older, grow up, and become adults.

3. Why?

Because too many adults don't have the skills they need to achieve their dreams and goals.

4. Why?

Because the education system failed them when they were students and didn't prepare them for the world beyond school.

5. Why?

Because school is often a one-size-fits-all environment where students who need something more or different are underserved.

6. Why?

Because one-size-fits-all tends to be more manageable for adults who are already trying to do their best without the resources they need.

7. Why are you an educator?

To honor and support the individual learning experience of every student to the best of my ability.

Intentional Summer Planning Protocol

This protocol is designed to help you plan your summer priorities to inform planning and decision-making. We recommend completing it with a partner who can help you articulate what's most important to you. You might try completing it several times throughout the spring to see how your summer vision evolves over time. See Chapter 5 for more resources on planning personal professional learning experiences.

Before the Protocol:

1. Write down all the things you want to accomplish this summer, both personally and professionally. Capture everything that comes to mind.

2. Put a star next to personal priorities and a circle around professional priorities.

3. Review your list and highlight the five priorities that are most important to you across both the personal and professional categories.

The Protocol:

1. Partner 1 lists what they want to do this summer personally and/or professionally.

2. Partner 2 repeats what they heard Partner 1 say about what's most important to them this summer.

3. Partner 1 reflects on what they've identified about their purpose this summer, ultimately framing it as a one-sentence summer purpose statement: "My purpose this summer is . . ."

4. Partner 2 repeats Partner 1's summer purpose statement.

5. Switch roles and repeat.

After the Protocol:

My professional purpose this summer is . . .

My personal purpose this summer is . . .

Brainstorm some things you might need to say no to this summer because they are not aligned to your purpose and/or could potentially get in the way of your priorities.

Reflect: How will it feel to say no? What will be difficult about this? How can your purpose help you?

Job Search Preparation Tool

Remember that while a prospective employer is interviewing you, you're also interviewing them. A school that wants to hire you should make a case for why they're a great fit for you, so remember that you're also evaluating them. Be prepared with research and questions to help you figure out whether their purpose is aligned with your own, as well as the other criteria that are important to you. If you know this is the right place for you, think about how you can prove that to the hiring committee by focusing on alignment of purpose and how you can help the school realize its vision for success, not just for your content knowledge and teaching experience. These prompts can help you prepare. You might also ask a colleague you know well and trust to complete it with you in mind to see what they envision as the right community for you so you can consider an alternative perspective, too. See Chapter 6 for more resources on finding a professional home that will help you keep your fire going.

What role have mission, vision, and/or core values played in the hiring process as you've experienced it? What have been the implications?

What are you looking for in a new school community? What kind of community do you need right now to fulfill your purpose?

How do you know that a school's purpose is a good match for your own?

What do you need to see and hear to evaluate a school where you would like to be hired? What products or activities should be part of the hiring process?

Does the school prioritize justice, equity, diversity, and inclusion? How do you know? Where do you see the evidence and impact of the school's commitment to anti-racism, or lack thereof?

Mentor Matching and Reflection Tool

This reflective tool can be used by administrators and teachers to identify new mentoring matches and build professional relationships grounded in complementary strengths, goals, and opportunities for growth. Mentors and mentees can also use these responses for the protocol that follows. See Chapters 5 and 7 for more mentoring resources.

1. What do you hope your students gain this school year?

2. What do you think you will need the most support with this year to reach this goal? (You might consider planning, classroom management, content knowledge, access to instructional/content resources, assessment/grading strategies, lesson modifications, or anything else.)

3. Think of a time where you got a piece of advice that you appreciated and were able to use. What was the advice, what made it useful, and how did you implement it?

4. What are your instructional strengths?

5. What do you think is the most effective way to provide feedback? What makes this method effective?

6. Think of a time where a mentor impacted your instructional practice. What did they do? How did they support you? What could have made this experience even more impactful?

Mentor/Mentee Initial Meeting Protocol:

◆ Mentee: Reflect on your hopes for the school year. What do you want your students to accomplish?

◆ Mentor: Share what you heard the mentee say with the goal of helping them create their professional goal.

◆ Mentee: Use what they heard the mentor say to create a goal statement. (You might use this template to help you get started: *By _____ I will _____, so my students _____.*)

◆ Mentor: Ask the mentee to share how they learn best, what kind of support they'd like to receive through mentoring, and any feedback or communication methods they prefer. Repeat what you heard and share what you commit to do.

◆ Open Discussion: Work together to plan what your mentoring relationship will look like. How often will you meet? When will you observe each other? How will you share feedback?

Modifying for Misalignment Tool

This tool is designed to help educators reflect on a unit or lesson that feels at odds with their purpose and identify possible ways to adapt the curriculum while maintaining alignment to learning standards. See Chapter 3 for more resources to support purposeful curriculum design.

1. What are your students learning? What standards are your students working toward?

2. Why are they learning this? (If your immediate answer is because it's mandated or on a state exam, ask yourself why that's the case. See The Five Whys tool for a protocol that may be helpful.)

3. List the learning experiences you want your students to engage in during this unit and/or lesson. How will you teach this content?

4. Assess the alignment of each experience to your purpose. Which ones are consistent with your purpose? Which ones seem to be in conflict?

5. For each learning experience that feels misaligned to your purpose, identify at least one alternative instructional approach to teaching this content.

6. What is within your locus of control that might help strengthen alignment to your purpose?

7. How might those changes impact your students and their learning experience?

Network Reflection Tool

In the TEDx Talks "Why I read a book a day (and why you should too): The law of 33%," Tai Lopez shares a framework for thinking about professional networks as composed of three groups of people:[2]

1. Those you look up to for inspiration and guidance because they have more experience or success than you (mentors, coaches, teachers).

2. Those who have the same level of experience and success as you (friends, teammates, co-teachers, happy hour buddies).

3. Those who look up to you for inspiration and guidance because you have more experience or success than them (mentees, coachees, student teachers, graduate students, preservice teachers, people who are considering becoming teachers, students, newer colleagues, first-year teachers).

We especially recommend using this tool to identify the folx you want to thank periodically or reach out to in case they're in need of support. See Chapter 7 for more resources on cultivating a supportive professional network.

Make a list of all the people in your professional community and sort them into one of these categories. Keep in mind that some people may have switched categories over time (as when a mentor becomes a peer, for example).

People You Learn From	People You Learn With	People You Teach

Once you've created your lists, consider the following questions:

What do you notice about your lists?

Does anything surprise you? What does looking at your community through this framework help you see that you might have been unaware of?

Are your lists fairly balanced, or do you have more people in some categories than others? Why do you think that is? What may have led you to have more mentors than mentees, for example?

Consider your current relationship to burnout. Do you see any connections between how you feel and the professional community you've cultivated? For example, are you at a point in your career where you need mentors who can help you explore new models for teaching and learning? Have you found a sustainable way to maintain your investment in the profession and want to share what you've learned with early-career teachers? Are you yearning for new teacher friends?

What actions does this framework inspire you to take? How would you like to grow your professional network so it provides the nourishment you need right now?

Planning Tool for a Sustainable Hiring Process

Hiring a new member to a community is a very important process and these resources can help ensure the school community is focused on hiring people not positions. See Chapter 6 for much more on the hiring process, especially the "Additional Considerations for Leaders" section.

Checklist Before Interviewing Candidates:

◆ Did you survey your current staff to see if they are committed to coming back for the next school year?

◆ Are there new positions you will need for the next school year?

  ◆ Is your school expanding in any way, adding a new grade, expecting more students with individual education plans, anticipating an increase in students who are multilingual learners, or anything else?

◆ Identify the stakeholders who are essential to have on the hiring committee. This should definitely include students!

◆ Pick a date and time to meet as a hiring committee.

Checklist to Set Up an Open House for Hiring:

◆ Find a date for an open house to bring candidates to your school. *If you are unable to bring candidates in, the open house can be through a virtual platform.*

  ◆ Check local universities and teacher prep programs to make sure the date of your open house does not interfere with anything the university has planned for teacher candidates.

  ◆ Check your district calendar to make sure the open house does not interfere with any district-wide teacher recruitment events.

◆ Create an agenda for the open house. Possibly include the following: tour of your school or campus, a chance to meet with students, a short interview, and so on.

◆ Create a notetaking document for your team to use when they interview candidates, so they can reflect on whether the candidate is a strong fit for your community.

◆ Create space for your team to reflect on the candidates to determine if they go to the next step of the interview process. All stakeholders should reflect, including students, staff, and/or parents.

Example Interview Questions:

◆ Educational philosophy:

   ◆ What is your purpose as an educator?

   ◆ What do you feel is the most impactful part of the role of an educator?

   ◆ What is your best quality as a teacher? Why is this quality important to you?

   ◆ What are you passionate about teaching in your content/specific area? What is one topic you are excited to teach your students?

◆ Curriculum and instruction:

   ◆ How do you plan for your students to master your content?

   ◆ How do you assess student learning?

   ◆ How do you make learning engaging and fun for students?

   ◆ What has been a lesson or idea you have enjoyed teaching students?

◆ Modifications:

   ◆ What do you think are the keys to modifying lessons/differentiating materials for all students?

   ◆ How do you determine which aspect(s) of a lesson to modify?

   ◆ Describe the process you go through when making modifications to a lesson.

- ◆ Overcoming challenges:

  - ◆ What is your approach to classroom management? What does your philosophy look like in day-to-day practice? Tell us about a time when your approach didn't work. What did you do? What did you learn?

  - ◆ Tell us about a time when you experienced a challenge, not necessarily at school. How did you handle it? What did you learn from it?

  - ◆ Who do you turn to when you need support? How do you ask for help?

- ◆ Feedback:

  - ◆ Describe a time when you modified a lesson based on feedback you received from a colleague, student, or supervisor. What did you change and how did it impact student learning?

  - ◆ What do you need to work on in your instruction? How do you know?

- ◆ Community:

  - ◆ Talk about a time or experience you've had working with someone or on a team toward a common goal. How did it go?

  - ◆ What does an ideal school community look like or feel like to you?

  - ◆ What is important to have as a school culture? How do you engage students outside of the classroom?

  - ◆ Where do you see yourself in five years?

Preparing for Conversations about Equity

As a principal, Meredith instituted monthly conversations about equity for her staff. These conversations are facilitated by a team of teachers with special training in this work. Here is a checklist Meredith created that came from reflecting on this work and was heavily influenced by Glenn E. Singleton and his book, *Courageous Conversations about Race*.[3] See also the resources in Chapter 1 on asserting a schoolwide equity stance and Chapter 5 for reading recommendations on anti-racism.

Considerations about purpose:

◆ Why do you want to engage your staff in conversations about equity?

◆ Is your entire staff ready to engage in conversations about equity? How do you know?

◆ Are these conversations voluntary or mandatory?

◆ What do you hope to achieve by facilitating conversations about equity with your staff?

◆ How will you ensure that student, family, and community voices are included in these conversations?

Considerations for facilitation:

◆ Who will facilitate? Is there someone on your staff with training for facilitating conversations about equity?

◆ Are there specific topics coming up that impact your community and need to be addressed in this forum?

◆ Do you have a space in your community where your entire staff can sit in a circle?

◆ If not, do you have multiple facilitators to support several concurrent conversations? Do they have or need training?

Considerations for the participant experience:

◆ What prompt will you use to start the conversation?

◆ Would it be helpful to share the prompt or topic ahead of time?

◆ How will you create and reinforce norms or community agreements to support the conversation?

◆ How will you open the conversation?

◆ How will you close the conversation?

Considerations for leaders:

◆ Will you participate?

　　◆ If so, what do you need to do to remove your "principal hat" so you can fully participate as an equal member of the conversation?

　　◆ If not, how will you message your decision to the staff so they understand why you are not participating?

◆ When and how will you address leadership or supervisory concerns that arise during the conversation, such as challenges to your school mission, values, or policies?

Professional Learning Reflection Tool

All learners need opportunities for synthesis, reflection, and closure. We always close the professional learning sessions we design and facilitate with a few minutes for educators to reflect on what they've learned and share their feedback to help us grow. This tool can be used for independent reflection and/or feedback on the learning experience. Even if your facilitator doesn't offer a structured time for reflection and feedback, you can still consolidate your own learning by answering these questions for yourself. See Chapter 5 for more resources to support professional learning experiences that reinforce adult learners' passions and purposes.

1. What are you taking away from today's session?

2. What action(s) are you planning to take as a result of today's session?

3. What worked well for you during today's session?

4. What could have made today's session even better?

5. Is there anything else you'd like to share?

Purposeful Planning Tool for Professional Learning

This tool is intended for professional learning leaders, designers, and facilitators to serve as an accompaniment to the planning materials you already use. See Chapter 5 for more resources to support professional learning experiences that fuel adult learners' professional fires.

1. What are your participants learning?

2. Why are they learning it?

3. How does this learning experience connect to your purpose as a leader in any way?

4. How does this learning experience further your, your school's, and your participants' purposes?

5. Where will learners have a voice, leadership, choice, and agency during their learning? How will they see the impact of this learning in their classrooms?

6. What will participants do when they gather together? Is the purpose of this gathering primarily to learn together? What structures have been established to support collaboration?

7. Where is the joy in this learning experience? How will you make learning engaging, exciting, and joyful for your participants?

8. As the facilitator, how will you model a lead learner mindset?

Purposeful Planning Tool for Units and Lessons

This tool is designed to serve as an accompaniment to the unit and lesson planning materials you already use. This can be completed before you write the lesson and/or unit to help you explore the connections between your purpose and your curriculum or it can be used as a reflection tool after the planning process. It can also be used by teams, co-teachers, or other professional learning communities that plan collaboratively. See Chapter 3 for more resources on purposeful curriculum design.

1. What are your students learning? What standards do you need to teach within the lesson and/or unit?

2. Why are they learning it?

3. List the learning experiences you want your students to engage in during this unit and/or lesson.

   For example, do you want them to perform an experiment, have a debate, reenact a play or chapter, solve a real-world problem, create and analyze graphs, etc.?

4. How does each learning experience connect to your purpose as an educator?

5. What learning experience are you most excited to facilitate ? Why?

6. Are there any learning experiences in tension with your purpose? If so, is there any way to adapt the experience to connect to your purpose?

Reflection Tool on Community Spaces for Collaboration

Physical space can be an integral factor in the extent to which adults in a school community are able to collaborate effectively. This tool can help educators and leaders evaluate how their physical spaces promote collaboration. Collaboration can spark a sense of passion and purpose in educators, prevent isolation, and build connections that drive continuous growth and development. A version of this resource also can be distributed as a staff survey to elicit input about how the staff lounge should be designed and used. See Chapter 7 for more resources on purposeful space design to cultivate a sense of belonging and community among adults.

1. How is space used in your school building? You might consider dedicated spaces for faculty, students, guidance staff, and classrooms.

2. How is your staff lounge designed for collaboration? You might consider table shape and configuration, available resources, technology, and food storage.

3. How are classrooms used and designed? You might consider the implications of shared classroom space and how classrooms are laid out in your school building to promote frequent collaboration.

184 APPENDIX REPRODUCIBLES

4. How are administrative office spaces designed for collaboration and to welcome students, families, visitors, and staff? You might consider which staff members share office space and what resources they need to be successful, such as the availability of necessary technology and water or other refreshments.

5. How do community members provide feedback on space usage in your school? You might consider ways students, families, and staff have a voice in space design and construction.

Reflection Tool for Burnout Factors

When using this tool, it may be tempting to immediately start tackling the factors contributing to your burnout, but as we recommend elsewhere in this book, give yourself permission to fully understand what the challenges are before you begin identifying solutions. Burnout doesn't have a quick fix, and trying to implement one that's unsuccessful might leave you even more exhausted, discouraged, and disillusioned. Instead, work to fully understand the burnout factors that are relevant to you before you start trying to fix them. See Chapter 2 for more resources on addressing the root causes of burnout.

How to use this tool:

1. Review the following burnout risk factors adapted from The Mayo Clinic[4] and mark all the factors that resonate with you, either because you have experienced them personally or think the teachers you supervise may be experiencing them.

2. Put a star next to the three most significant factors in your experience and use the space below that item to write down a memory or story that captures what that experience feels like.

3. Connect with someone who cares about you and share your story. Ask your partner to simply listen and help you understand your experience without trying to solve the problem or make you feel better. Allow your feelings to be validated. You might discover even more elements of your experience you want to capture. Feel free to add to your written memory afterward and to repeat this activity with other stories you want to share.

◆ A feeling that you have little or no control over your work, including the decisions that affect your job, your schedule, and access to the resources you need.

◆ A lack of clarity about what's expected of you, such as who's in charge and how you're being evaluated.

◆ A dysfunctional workplace where bullying is tolerated, colleagues undermine each other, or you feel micromanaged.

◆ A loss of equilibrium, where the work feels monotonous or chaotic, and you constantly have to maintain high energy levels to be productive.

◆ A lack of support that leads to isolation, siloing you in your classroom or office with a sense you have to fend for yourself and have no one to turn to.

◆ A lack of work-life balance, where you must spend so much time on your work that you don't have energy for family or friends.

Reflection Tool for Designing Classroom Systems

When thinking about your classroom systems, you want to ensure that the way you run your classroom is aligned with your purpose so you can lead your learners with authenticity, consistency, and integrity. Think about how your systems are implemented in your classroom to ensure students are aware of the expectations. When the expectations are consistent and transparent for students and connect to your passion, all students—and you!—can be successful. This tool is designed to get you started in thinking about your classroom systems. You can use these prompts to inspire your exploration of other systems not explicitly referenced here.

While this resource might be especially useful for early-career educators who are working to design their classroom environments, we've found that more experienced teachers also benefit from reflecting on their classroom systems each year to identify what's already working well and what might work even better for students. Additionally, teacher teams that use the same classroom systems can work through the tool together. See Chapter 4 for more resources on designing purposeful classroom systems to support transformative learning experiences.

1. How do students know what the daily agenda or lesson structure is?

2. What do students experience at the beginning of class? How do they enter your classroom? How do they know that the learning experience has begun?

3. How do students get the materials they need to be successful during the lesson?

4. How do students know when and how to transition to different parts of the lesson?

5. What does collaboration look like in your classroom? How do students know what to do and how to do it?

Sample poster from Meredith's classroom to support collaborative work:

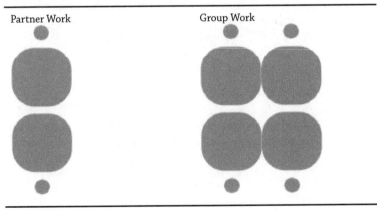

Sample Student Feedback Survey

When Rebekah was a classroom teacher, she invited her students to complete anonymous surveys at the end of every unit as well as midyear and at the end of the school year to share their feedback. After students submitted their surveys, she gathered the data, evaluated it for trends, and then composed her response to her students about what she'd learned from them and what changes she was going to make as a result. Here's the actual survey Rebekah's students completed at the end of the year on the weekly poetry presentations they conducted. See Chapter 4 for more resources on incorporating student voice in instruction.

Anonymous Poetry Presentation Feedback Survey
Circle the number that corresponds to how you feel about each of the following statements.

1	2	3	4	5
Strongly disagree	Disagree	Neutral	Agree	Strongly agree

1. I enjoy teaching poetry to the class.

     1   2   3   4   5

2. I enjoy being part of the audience when another group is teaching.

     1   2   3   4   5

3. I believe the poetry presentations have helped me to be a better reader.

     1   2   3   4   5

4. I believe the poetry response papers have helped me to be a better writer.

     1   2   3   4   5

5. I understand poetry more now than I did at the beginning of the year.

     1   2   3   4   5

6. Poetry presentations have helped me to improve my scores on the AP poetry essay.

1   2   3   4   5

7. I would do an additional poetry presentation for extra credit.

1   2   3   4   5

8. The lessons on writing prompts and lesson planning helped me prepare my presentation.

1   2   3   4   5

9. The poetry presentations have helped improve my ability to compare and contrast.

1   2   3   4   5

10. I recommend that poetry presentations continue to be part of this class next year.

1   2   3   4   5

11. Here's what I like about poetry presentations:

12. Here's what would improve poetry presentations, in my opinion:

13. Is there anything else you'd like to share?

Staff Member Community Involvement Survey

Use this survey to help establish opportunities for teachers to connect with the school community beyond their classrooms and offices when possible and to identify potential leadership roles. See Chapters 6 and 7 for more resources on cultivating a sense of belonging and community among staff members.

1. From a scale of 1 to 10 (1 = not at all and 10 = very connected), how connected do you feel to our community? Explain your response.

2. What are things you enjoy doing outside of school that you think your students may enjoy? *For example, do you work out, cook, read, play sports, meditate, and so on?*

3. How can you share this passion with your students within your position? *For example, can you begin your class or sessions with students meditating?*

4. How can you share this passion with your students outside of your specific role? *For example, can you start a club, plan an event for students after school or during lunch, and so on?*

5. Are there any initiatives within our school community that you want to join? What are they and why? *For example, mentoring a teacher, joining a committee, and so on.*

Would you be interested in being a part of the following activities?

1	2	3	4	5
Not at all interested	Slightly interested	Neutral	Interested	Very interested

1. I would enjoy mentoring a teacher.

       1   2   3   4   5

2. I would like to coach a sports team.

       1   2   3   4   5

3. I would like to be an advisor for student government.

       1   2   3   4   5

4. I would like to create an after-school club for students.

       1   2   3   4   5

5. I would like to lead grade team.

       1   2   3   4   5

6. I would like to lead a department team.

       1   2   3   4   5

7. I would like to analyze student data for teams to use in their meetings.

       1   2   3   4   5

8. I would like to be a part of the school's equity team.

       1   2   3   4   5

9. I would like to be the advisor for the school's restorative justice team.

       1   2   3   4   5

10. I would like to be the advisor for the school's newspaper.

       1   2   3   4   5

Teacher-Led Inquiry Cycle for Professional Development

One way to ensure teachers are the lead learners in professional development is to set up structures in an inquiry cycle to ensure there is teacher choice and the learning is teacher-driven. See Chapter 5 for more resources on teacher-led professional learning experiences.

The prep work:

◆ Create an instructional focus for the school while incorporating the feedback from the stakeholders within your community, integrating the district focus as applicable.

◆ Define what the instructional focus will look like, sound like, and feel like within classrooms.

◆ Evaluate the instructional focus using a video of instruction that is not from your school community.

◆ Evaluate the instructional focus using a lesson plan that is not from your school community.

◆ Break the instructional focus up into specific pillars that can drive professional learning communities (PLCs).

◆ Set up your PLCs based on these pillars and allow your teacher groups to choose their specific focus.

Conduct your inquiry cycles:

1. Goal setting and assessment

- Review standards and identify specific student skills you want to assess.
- Create an assessment that evaluates your students' performance in connection to these standards.
- Review the assessment results with a unified rubric and identify a skill you want to address through the following inquiry cycle.

2. Instructional strategy focus

- Research instructional strategies that specifically help students improve their focus skill.
- Create a lesson that incorporates this instructional strategy.
- Receive peer feedback on the lesson plan.
- Implement the lesson and collect student work.
- Continue to implement the instructional strategy as frequently as possible.

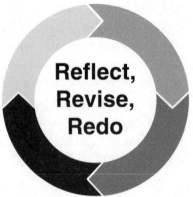

Reflect,
Revise,
Redo

Teacher-Led Inquiry Cycle for Professional Development

4. Debrief intervisitations

- Norm how to take low-inference notes in a classroom.
- Visit classrooms and take low-inference notes.
- Categorize the low-inference notes to discover trends on what teacher moves are effective in helping students succeed on the focus skill.

3. Looking at student work

- Identify student work that represents a diverse group of student learners. This should include students with individualized education plans; students who are multilingual learners; students who exceeded, are just meeting, or have not yet met expectations.
- Evaluate this work with a group of educators based on a normed rubric.
- Discuss trends, reflect on the impact of the instructional strategy, and discuss potential next steps.

Time Management Tool

The roles and responsibilities of anyone who works in a school are never-ending, and there are so many times when our to-do lists feel endless. When we get overwhelmed, we can lose track of our purpose easily and our passion can get stripped away. This tool is meant to help you stay focused on what you want to accomplish to be productive in alignment with your purpose. It can also be used by administrative and teacher teams to plan how they will use their time to accomplish a collective goal or project. See Chapter 2 for more tools for addressing the root causes of burnout.

What is your goal for the week? *This can be within or outside of your classroom.*

List all the things you *must* get done to reach this goal:

List all the things you *want* to get done to reach this goal:

Break down your week: Use the chart below to ensure your time is focused throughout the day.

Teachers might want to include:

◆ Tasks necessary for achieving your weekly goal.

◆ Teaching periods.

◆ Prep periods. (Write down specifically what you hope to accomplish in these periods.)

◆ Professional responsibilities.

◆ Lunch.

◆ Family outreach.

◆ Co-planning or other collaborative work time.

◆ Anything else you spend time on during the work week.

Leaders might want to include:

◆ Tasks necessary for achieving your weekly goal.

◆ Classroom observations.

◆ Crafting and delivering feedback to teachers and staff.

◆ Administrative meetings.

◆ Teacher meetings.

◆ Family outreach.

◆ Anything else you spend time on during the work week.

WEEKLY PLAN

Period or block	Monday	Tuesday	Wednesday	Thursday	Friday
1					
2					
3					
4					
5					
6					
7					
8					
9					
10					

Notes

1. Mayo Clinic Staff (2021). Job burnout: how to spot it and take action. Mayo Clinic (21 June). https://www.mayoclinic.org/healthy-lifestyle/adult-health/in-depth/burnout/art-20046642 (accessed 25 November 2022).
2. Lopez, T. (2015). Why I read a book a day (and why you should too): the law of 33%. TEDx Talks (15 January). https://youtu.be/7bB_fVDlvhc (accessed 25 November 2022).
3. Singleton, G.E. (2015). *Courageous Conversations about Race: A Field Guide for Achieving Equity in Schools*. Thousand Oaks, CA: Corwin.
4. Mayo Clinic Staff. (2021). Job burnout: how to spot it and take action. Mayo Clinic (21 June). https://www.mayoclinic.org/healthy-lifestyle/adult-health/in-depth/burnout/art-20046642 (accessed 25 November 2022).

Acknowledgments

Thank you to Jamal Solomon for believing in us without even knowing us yet; Lawrence Goldberg, Malla Haridat, Stephen Motika, and Dr. Kristen Turner for invaluable advice about the business of books; Shelby Sprung for providing us with a writing oasis; and the team members at Jossey-Bass and Wiley who made this book possible. We didn't know what we didn't know, and we're so grateful that all of you were there to guide us.

Thank you to the mentors and colleagues who generously volunteered their time to read early editions of this book and provide feedback: Elena Aguilar, Carlos Beato, Jeffrey Garrett, Marshall George, Alexis Goldberg, Bil Johnson, Jessica Murnane, Ivelisse Ramos, Shelby Sprung, Kristen Turner, David Weinberg, and Carolyn Yaffe. Your time and support mean the world to us.

Thank you to the current and former students who gave us permission to include their wise words about teaching and learning in this book: Michael Barrientos, Edward Chan, Cherelinis Filpo, Martha Mendoza, Leianna Santos, Emmy Shoaf, Eli Sookhansingh, and Tevin Williams. You are the reason we do this work.

Thank you to Lawrence Pendergast, Matthew Willoughby, and Madhu Narayanan for seeing our leadership potential before we did and entrusting us with the responsibilities and experiences that allowed us to explore our passions, deepen our understanding of our purpose, and tackle important and inspiring teaching and learning challenges. Your impact lives on so many pages of this book.

Meredith's Turn

Thank you to all of the people who have cared for me and this book. My husband and rock, Mike: you have supported me throughout this entire process and it is what has truly led to me accomplishing this goal in life. Max and Luke, your encouragement and disbelief that your mom is going to be an author pushes me on a daily basis. Thank you to my parents, Stephan and Marla Parmett, my brother, sister-in-law, and nephew, Justin, Helen, and Nakobe Morgan Parmett, and the extended Parmett, Stier, and Matson families. To all my friends who have believed in me throughout my life. You have lifted me up at times when I needed you most, you have given me advice, watched my children, and lent me a shoulder to cry on and laughed or snorted with me in so many happy times. I am also so thankful for my professional network and current and past students who lift me up every day and have inspired so much of this book. Lastly, this book and dream has come true because of the strength that I got from my beloved mother, my guiding light. Nancy, your light shines through this book. I love you.

Rebekah's Turn

To the extended Shoaf, Dugoni, and Burnside families: thank you for making me who I am and rooting me on as I continue to become, especially my sister Elizabeth, who is my biggest cheerleader, best customer, and personal hero. Thank you to Rachel Bello, Liz Madans, and all of my friends—in education and otherwise—who have supported me in so many ways throughout the writing of this book, which also means through the pandemic. Ultimately, there would be no fire within me without my late grandmother Mary Leposky Dugoni. She lit the match, my parents Dave and Diane Shoaf added the kindling, and my students and colleagues continue to fan the flames.

Our Turn

Finally and most importantly, thank you to the current and former students, staff, and faculty at the Urban Assembly School of Design and Construction. In every sense, this book would not exist without you.

About the Authors

Meredith Matson is a New York City principal at a small theme-based high school with the mission of preparing students for college and beyond. Throughout her 21-year career as an educator, she taught for 11 years, was an assistant principal for five years, and has been a principal for the past five years. During her experience within the classroom, she was a mentor to numerous new teachers and student teachers, she co-led professional development, was the history department leader and the tenth grade team leader, and an active member of the school leadership team. In all her interactions with students and colleagues, her philosophy of promoting high expectations, relationship-building, and spaces to reflect is at the core of her work. Meredith studied secondary education and sociology at the University of Vermont and earned her master's degree in School Building Leadership at Pace University. She considers herself a lifelong learner and earned her School District Leader certificate at Molloy College while writing this book. She lives in Baldwin, New York with her husband Mike and her two sons, Max (11) and Luke (8), and their dog Marcy. Learn more and contact her at meredithmatson.com.

Rebekah Shoaf is a New York City-based educational consultant and the founder and owner of Boogie Down Books, a bookstore-without-walls® for kids, teens, families, and educators in the Bronx and beyond, and What If Schools, an educational consultancy. Throughout her 20-year career in education she has served as a high school English teacher, graduate professor, instructional and leadership coach, professional development facilitator, and curriculum designer. A Miami native, Rebekah is a lifelong bookworm, a product of public and independent schools, a *magna cum laude* graduate of Harvard University, an alum of the Chef's Training Program at the Natural Gourmet Institute, the owner of a pink Vespa, and an aunt to six budding bibliophiles. Learn more and contact her at rebekahshoaf.com.

Index